Transformational Grammar
and the Teacher of English

Transformational Grammar
and the
Teacher
of English

Owen Thomas

Indiana University

Holt, Rinehart and Winston, Inc.

NEW YORK, CHICAGO, SAN FRANCISCO, TORONTO, LONDON

To E. K. T.

Preface

This book is a pedagogical rather than a scientific grammar. (The significance of this distinction is discussed in Chapter 1.) Specifically, it seeks to describe those aspects of transformational grammar that, in my opinion, have the greatest relevance for teachers and prospective teachers of English. It is designed so that it may be used as a text, by departments of English and schools of education, but I believe it can also be used independently by teachers who have completed their formal education. In short, it is my hope that teachers will learn something valuable about the nature of English from this text and that this knowledge will improve their teaching and help their students.

But as a teacher whom I admire has said, I must warn you that I am a pedagogue and not a linguist. To put it another way, I am personally and professionally interested in the problems of teaching English and only peripherally interested in the problems of theoretical linguists. To achieve my primary aim in the best way I know how, I must risk offending those whose professional interest is in theory. I admire and respect them, but there is little I can do to enlighten them. Our problems are different.

Finally, I want to thank a few of the many people who have helped me with this book. First, I thank my several classes of both experienced and prospective teachers who worked through various stages of the book with me. Second, I acknowledge the assistance of particular individuals who have given encouragement and advice, specifically, Harold B. Allen who first suggested that I write the book; Andreas Koutsoudas, whose theoretical knowledge and patience helped me in many particular ways; and Fred Householder and Paul Schachter, both of whom read the manuscript in its entirety and smoothed out many infelicities of diction (the errors and infelicities that remain are, of course, my

responsibility). Third, I thank my typist, Mrs. Phyllis
Fletcher, who is remarkable for both her conscientiousness
and her even temper. And last, I thank my wife—Ellen K.
Thomas. Every word of this book owes something to her
humor, her wisdom, and her understanding.

O. T.

Bloomington, Indiana
September 1965

Contents

ix

Transformational Grammar and the Teacher of English

⟨1⟩

New Terms and Old Ideas

And far across the hills they went
In that new world which is the old.

TENNYSON, *The Day-dream.*

Transformational grammar is the term popularly applied to the most recent major development in American linguistics. The term came into prominence in 1957 when Noam Chomsky, a professor of linguistics at the Massachusetts Institute of Technology, published *Syntactic Structures*, which presents a brief and somewhat technical discussion of the original form of the theory. Since that time many linguists and educators have recognized the theory as one of the most significant developments in the study of language in this generation. The original theory has undergone one major and several minor revisions, and certainly additional revisions are being made now and will continue to be made during the years ahead. Nonetheless, there is widespread agreement among linguists that both the basis and the general outline of the theory are established. And linguists also agree that transformational grammar has significant application to the teaching of all languages, including English, at all grade levels and to both native and nonnative speakers.

But teachers and prospective teachers of English generally feel that transformational grammar is both esoteric and forbidding. Most teachers have probably read one or more of the articles that attempt to explain the theory,

1

but nothing so brief as an article can give more than a general idea, and no article can do more than whet a teacher's intellectual appetite. Many teachers have heard discussions of the theory at meetings of various professional societies, but like the articles, such discussions do not pretend to be exhaustive. A few teachers have enrolled in special institutes sponsored by the National Council of Teachers of English or by the Linguistic Society of America, and these fortunate few have been able to gain a better understanding of the nature and value of transformational grammar. But the many demands on the time of teachers prevent such institutes from being a reasonable answer to the problem of understanding the theory. And finally, a handful of very brave teachers have, on their own, worked through such books as Emmon Bach's *An Introduction to Transformational Grammars*, and even through *Syntactic Structures* itself, but this small group of teachers has generally had the linguistic training required for an understanding of these books.

In short, the overwhelming majority of teachers are confused and many are even apprehensive. Quite reasonably, both teachers and prospective teachers of English are asking a number of significant questions. What is the difference between transformational grammar and the kind that linguists were talking about four or five years ago? How do we know there won't be another kind of grammar in another five or ten years? Must a teacher spend two or three years studying linguistics before he is prepared to teach grammar in the elementary and secondary schools? How does transformational grammar apply to the teaching of English? If the teachers have such a difficult time understanding this new grammar, how can they possibly teach it to students? Does transformational grammar simply offer some new terms for what are really old ideas?

These are vitally important questions which teachers of English have a right to ask and which linguists interested in their problems have an obligation to answer. But as with all such questions, the answers are not always immediately obvious, even to linguists who have been concerned with these problems for years. Some answers, to be sure, can be stated definitively, but others are much more tentative. Some can be given outright, but the most important of them require at least a partial understanding of some linguistic terms.

1.1   SOME BASIC TERMS

Before looking at the details of transformational grammar, we must first place the theory—at least approximately—in the context of other linguistic theories. This requires that we define some basic terms and establish some basic distinctions. In particular, we must give a brief definition of **linguistics**, and we must present a brief outline of the history of English grammatical studies. To do this, we must also define the distinctions between the following pairs of terms:

1. Scientific grammar and pedagogical grammar.
2. Competence and performance.
3. Transformational and generative.
4. Syntax and semantics.
5. States and operations.

When we have defined the distinctions, we will then be able to ask some basic questions about the nature and function of grammar, and this will provide a framework for our investigation of transformational theory and its applications to teaching.

Linguistics.   The term linguistics refers to the scientific study of language. Things scientific were formerly anathema to teachers who were by disposition more concerned with the humanistic values of literature and writing. But most teachers now realize that the arts and sciences are interdependent both in the academic world and in life itself.

Like most fields of study, linguistics can be divided into many areas. Some linguists, for example, are interested in cataloguing and describing various features of languages, just as some botanists prefer to catalogue and describe plants. Other linguists are interested in the history of various languages and language families, just as some anthropologists are primarily interested in tracing the history of various families of mankind. Still other linguists are concerned with the interrelationships between language and society, or language and learning, or language and intelligence, just as sociologists, educational theorists, and psychologists are interested in similar questions. And finally, some few linguists are interested in general theories of language, just as some physicists are interested in theories that explain the operations of the universe. No single linguist is trained in all these fields, and, quite obviously, no teacher of English need become expert in any one of them.

One group of linguists has come to be called the **transformationalists**. They are primarily concerned with the theory of language. More particularly, they want to describe a general theory of grammar which will precisely specify "the form that a grammar may assume"[1] and will also provide a procedure for evaluating two or more grammars in order to determine which offers the best description of a particular language.

Scientific Grammar and Pedagogical Grammar. Transformationalists hope to specify a "scientific grammar" which offers a logical, complete, and self-consistent explanation for the way any particular language operates. We may get some idea of what this means by looking at two sentences that Chomsky has frequently used for illustrative purposes:[2]

Sentence 1.1   John is easy to please.

Sentence 1.2   John is eager to please.

---

[1] Noam Chomsky, "Explanatory Models in Linguistics," in Ernest Nagel and Others, eds., *Logic Methodology and Philosophy of Science* (Stanford, California, Stanford University Press, 1962), p. 535.

[2] *Ibid.*, p. 532.

All mature native speakers of English recognize that the underlying forms of these two sentences are different. The difference becomes more obvious when we try to rearrange the sentences. Thus, we can say *It was easy for us to please John*, but we cannot say **It was eager for us to please John*.[3] On the other hand, we can say *He was eager to please us*, but not **He was easy to please us*. In English, there are many such cases. A scientific grammar, among other things, aims at providing a generalized explanation for all these cases. Moreover, it also aims at showing the relationship between these kinds of constructions and hundreds of others that are similar but not identical in form. In brief, a scientific grammar is concerned with logical generalizations about the way language operates.

By its very nature, a scientific grammar is quite different from a "pedagogical grammar" such as a teacher wants to use in a classroom with students. On the other hand, it seems apparent that any pedagogical grammar must be based on the best available scientific grammar.

There are many varieties of pedagogical grammar. For example, a grammar designed to instruct a native speaker of English in his own language, even if that speaker is only a young child, will be significantly different from one designed to teach English to a native speaker of German. And since German and English are members of the same "language family," this second grammar would be quite different from one designed to teach English to a native speaker of Japanese. Similarly, a pedagogical grammar which serves as a basis for an explanation of how people "understand" sentences they hear or read would be different from one designed to help explain how people "produce" the sentences they speak.

These distinctions suggest why the title of this book refers to the "teacher" rather than to the "teaching" of

---

[3] The linguistic convention of placing an asterisk (*) in front of a sentence that is not grammatical—or as is sometimes said, that is not "well formed"—is used throughout this text. To facilitate location of cross references, all illustrative sentences are numbered consecutively through each chapter, i.e., Sentence 1.1, Sentence 1.2, Sentence 1.3, and so on.

English. All teachers of English need to be aware of the best available scientific description of language; they need, in short, to know the theory. But they will not all use the theory and the description in the same way when it comes to teaching English.

Competence and Performance. The distinction between scientific and pedagogical grammars also relates to one between "competence" and "performance." And this latter distinction can also be viewed in many ways. By the time a child is five or six, he has been exposed to a wide variety of linguistic experiences. He has heard hundreds of thousands of sentences, most of them well formed but many of them not completely well formed (such as, for example, those from his playmates). He has spoken thousands of sentences of his own; he has been encouraged by such things as smiles from parents and by getting what he asks for when he makes a request; he has occasionally been corrected when he makes mistakes. On the basis of these and many other kinds of experiences, he has—in some fashion almost completely unknown to linguists and psychologists —constructed a grammar of his language that permits him to produce thousands of sentences that he has never, in fact, heard. In other words, every child somehow learns to make generalizations about language on the basis of his exposure to linguistic experiences of various kinds. More precisely, on the basis of being exposed to almost random and arbitrary linguistic data, every child develops a certain degree of linguistic "competence." No one yet knows precisely how to describe this competence, since it cannot be observed directly. All that we can observe is a speaker's "performance"; that is, the sentences he actually produces. And these can be influenced by a wide variety of factors, many of them not connected with linguistics at all. For example, the speech of any native speaker will be influenced by such things as whether he is tired, or embarrassed, or in a hurry. Yet these things affect only the performance of the speaker; his linguistic competence remains unaffected by them. On the other hand, linguistic competence gener-

ally increases, up to a point, as a speaker grows older. But
this competence may be different from a change in performance that is brought about, for example, when a
child moves from one part of the country to another and
abandons the pronunciation common in the old area for
that common in the new.

All this means, of course, that competence is a very difficult thing to understand. Certainly all attempts to describe "verbal behavior" on the basis of external factors
have been unsuccessful.[4] In spite of literally thousands of
years of investigating language, we do not know very much
about the way speakers actually produce sentences.

It is for this reason that linguists use the methods of
modern symbolic logic in constructing grammars. In effect
they are saying, "Since we can't describe the 'competence' of a native speaker, then we can at least try to construct a grammar that does all the important things a native speaker does." The developments during the twentieth
century in the theory of symbolic logic and in the theory of
proof provide a means of constructing such a grammar.

No one claims that such a "logical" or scientific grammar is a duplicate of the grammar which enables a native
speaker to produce sentences. In fact, the chances that
such a grammar is a duplicate are so small as to be insignificant. But at least at this time, and probably for some
time to come, a logical grammar is the closest thing we
have to "natural" or "intuitive" grammar. This is one reason why teachers of English should be familiar with transformational grammar, and it is also one reason why such a
grammar should underlie any instruction in the English
language at any grade level.

Transformational and Generative.   The term transformational, as we have been using it thus far, is somewhat
imprecise. More accurately, we should say "transformational generative grammar." And the key term here is **gen-**

---

[4] See Chomsky's review of B. F. Skinner's *Verbal Behavior* which ap-
peared in *Language*, Vol. 35 (January-March, 1959), pp. 26-58.

erative. Briefly, a generative grammar is one that contains a list of symbols, including—for example—English words, and a list of rules for combining these symbols in various ways to produce every English sentence.[5] Such a grammar is said to "generate" or to "enumerate" all the possible sentences in a language. "To generate," however, does not mean "to produce." The number of sentences in English is potentially infinite, as we shall note more fully in later chapters. No speaker of English could possibly *produce* this infinite number of sentences. But all speakers have some method of *understanding* completely novel sentences never spoken before, which means that they must have a way of "determining" all of the infinite number of sentences. In other words, rules that generate or determine are actually generalizations about language which permit a native speaker, among other things, to evaluate the grammaticality of any novel sentence.

We can illustrate these facts with relative ease. Most, if not all, of the following sentences are novel; that is, they have never been spoken or written before:

Sentence 1.3   My sister, an eminent orthodontist, is inordinately fond of pickled snails.

Sentence 1.4   Gertrude, why are you throwing those party hats into the river?

Sentence 1.5   Every college in Australia should offer a course in how to prepare peanut butter.

The examples are all perfectly good English sentences, and we can "understand" what they mean even though they are probably unique. However, we also recognize that the following sentences, which we have all heard, are not well-formed sentences in the socially prestigious dialect:

Sentence 1.6   *He don't got none.

Sentence 1.7   *Me and him did it.

Sentence 1.8   *He hadn't ought to do it.

---

[5] Technically, the "lists" are actually "sets" as logicians and mathematicians use this term.

Any grammar, through its generative or enumerative power, should tell us why the first three sentences, though novel, are nonetheless grammatical. The second three sentences are not part of the prestige dialect but belong rather to the "grammar" of a socially disadvantaged dialect.

The term **transformation** is more difficult to describe at this point, although the definition will become obvious in later chapters. Briefly, however, we may say that a transformation is a rule which rearranges various elements that occur in English sentences. In terms of our earlier definition of a generative grammar as consisting of a set of symbols and a set of rules, we may say that transformations are rules which combine the symbols in various ways. The distinction between "transformational" and "generative" is thus an important one, but the term "transformational generative grammar" is so cumbersome that we shall adopt the shorter and more popular term, "transformational grammar," throughout this text.

The History of Grammar. We can now place transformational grammar in relation to earlier forms of grammar. Briefly, these earlier forms can be divided into three main classes: (1) traditional, (2) comparative and historical, and (3) structural and descriptive.

English traditional grammar has its roots in the Greek grammar of Dionysius Thrax (c. 200 B.C.) and in the Latin grammars of Donatus (c. 400 A.D.) and Priscian (c. 600 A.D.). The methodology of these classical grammarians was adopted by the grammarians of eighteenth century England, most notably Joseph Priestly, Robert Lowth, George Campbell, and Lindley Murray. The grammars of these men are all based on the assumption that "the structure of various languages, and especially of Latin, embodies universally valid canons of logic."[6]

Briefly, the grammarians of eighteenth century England sought to discover logical rules of syntax and usage.

---

[6] Leonard Bloomfield, *Language* (New York, Holt, Rinehart and Winston, Inc., 1933), p. 6.

They generally assumed that Latin was the most logical of languages, and they consequently based their rules for English on Latin models. These rules were almost invariably prescriptive; that is, they dictated precisely the usage to be followed by all speakers and writers. The early English grammarians either overlooked the fact that all languages change, or else they considered such change as corruption. Yet for all their appeals to "classical logic" in language, they also displayed a heavy reliance on "intuition" in discovering the rules. In other words, not only did they base their rules for English partly on the rules for Latin, but partly also on their intuition about what was correct in their own language. Consequently, we must recognize that many of their "rules" are actually explanations of intuition.

Reliance on intuition, or more particularly, on the intuition of a native speaker, is probably essential in studying language. Equally essential is the attempt to discover the logic of any language (although this logic may be different from classical logic). The theoretical basis of traditional grammar, therefore, is solid and, as we shall see in later chapters, is nearly identical to the basis of transformational grammar. On the other hand, the traditional grammarians were largely unaware of certain linguistic facts, and this lack of awareness can be seen in the applications of their theories to practical problems.

Before looking at these linguistic facts, we should note that modern "school grammars," such as those most widely used in elementary and secondary schools today, are based almost exclusively on the models of the eighteenth century English grammarians. They are largely prescriptive, and their "explanations" of such things as agreement and the passive voice are based upon an intuitive perception of the structure of English. However, they too ignore many linguistic facts, and most importantly and unfortunately, they rarely give any indication for the theoretical basis of grammatical rules.

While the English grammarians of the eighteenth century were formulating their prescriptive rules, many grammarians in France and Germany were looking at language more speculatively. More particularly, they rediscovered Panini's magnificent grammar of Sanskrit, the ancient literary dialect of India, which was probably written late in the fourth century, B.C. Sanskrit bore a strong resemblance not only to Latin and Greek but also to German and English and even to Russian. This led many grammarians to suggest, at first tentatively but then with increasing conviction, that most modern European languages as well as Sanskrit and classical Latin and Greek derive historically from some common source. Briefly, these grammarians noted one apparently universal linguistic fact: all languages change.

This observation led to two kinds of study: comparative and historical. Many grammarians began a wide investigation of various languages, looking for similarities or, as they are called, **cognate forms**. They discovered some striking facts. The English word *mother* has cognates in Greek (*mētēr*), Latin (*māter*), Russian (*mat'*), and German (*Mutter*). They also discovered that within the large family of languages which includes Sanskrit, Greek, Latin, Russian, German, and English, there are several smaller families. Take, for example, the English word *drink*:[7]

Germanic Group	Romance Group	Slavic Group	
English *drink*	French *boire*	Russian	*pit'*
Dutch *drinken*	Italian *bere*	Polish	*pic'*
German *trinken*	Spanish *beber*	Bohemian	*piti*
Danish *drikke*		Serbian	*piti*
Swedish *dricka*			

Table 1.1   To drink.

As this chart indicates, there are strong similarities among the words in the three groups. (The *c* in the Polish word *pic'* is pronounced like the *-ts* ending on the English word *cats.*) English belongs to the Germanic Group, and the Ger-

---

[7] *Ibid.*, p. 10.

manic, Romance, and Slavic Groups are all part of a larger language family which is generally called **Indo-European**.

At the same time that some grammarians were making comparative studies, others were tracing the history of particular languages as far back as written records permitted. The chief result of this study, for students of English, was the elaborate description of Old and Middle English. Like modern German, Old English had masculine, feminine, and neuter genders that were "grammatical" rather than "logical"; for example, the word *stān* ("stone") was masculine and the word *giefu* ("gift") was feminine. Nouns could be either "strong" or "weak," depending on whether the stem ended in a vowel or consonant, and there were four distinct declensions for the strong nouns. Each declension had separate singular and plural forms for each of four cases: nominative, genitive, dative, and accusative. In addition, adjectives also had strong and weak, and masculine, feminine, and neuter forms. The strong declension of adjectives even had a fifth case: the instrumental. The definite article was also fully inflected; Old English had eleven separate forms for the word *the*. There were six major classes of strong verbs, each with distinctive endings, as well as a large class of weak verbs and a special class of "reduplicating verbs." In short, Old English was a highly inflected language.

Middle English, the language of Chaucer, had far fewer inflections. As a consequence, word order became increasingly important. And this trend away from inflections and toward a more rigid word order has continued into modern English. We can, therefore, speak of a contrast between inflected and positional languages. And with this distinction in mind, we can look back at the works of the eighteenth century English grammarians. Their descriptions of English, a positional language, were based on models of Greek and Latin, which are inflected languages. Their descriptions, therefore, were almost certain to be misleading and even at variance with their own intuition.

The historical and comparative grammarians were so preoccupied with their research that they failed to look

closely at the language around them. It was not until the
nineteenth century that linguists made any serious attempt to describe precisely the form of Modern English.
And it was not until the early part of the twentieth century
that linguists developed increasingly precise tools of description. The late nineteenth and early twentieth centuries
saw some major compilations of linguistic data relating to
Modern English. Many of these compilations were the work
of non-English scholars, perhaps the most notable of whom
is the Dane, Otto Jespersen. Jespersen and similar grammarians also attempted to classify their data into syntactically significant categories, but they rarely attempted to
describe the data in any very precise and logically acceptable way. In short, like the historical grammarians before
them, they were so preoccupied with collecting and cataloguing data that they apparently had neither the time nor
the inclination to make a logical analysis of the data.

This task was reserved for the descriptive and structural grammarians of the twentieth century. The most
notable of the early descriptivists were Leonard Bloomfield and Edward Sapir. Briefly, they sought to describe
present-day English not as people think it "should be" but
as it actually is. We must note that they were not primarily
concerned with operations in language; they were not at-
tempting to explain intuition. Rather they, and even more
particularly their followers, were looking for methods of
describing language that were free of human error and
subjective judgments. They sought to make the study of
language as objective as the study of physics and chemistry. They wanted to bring rigor to linguistics.

The achievements of the structuralists are many. Perhaps most important, they noted that the study of language
can and should be divided into two parts: syntax and semantics.

Syntax and Semantics. Generally speaking, **syntax** refers to the structure of language and **semantics** refers to
meaning. One function of the study of syntax, according
to many modern linguists, is to provide a basis for the study

of semantics. In other words, form in language is one way
of getting at meaning in language or, as a linguist would
say, "form underlies meaning." As a consequence of this
fact, many linguists assume (and we shall return to this
assumption later) that the study of syntax must precede
the study of semantics and that any appeal to semantics
in studying syntax is wrong. They conceived the notion of
syntactic levels in language and developed new terms to
describe these levels. They also placed increasing emphasis
on the spoken language as opposed to the written language.
And they insisted that there is no *single* standard of usage
and correctness in language.

The descriptivists were—and continue to be—widely
misunderstood. They were unfairly accused of advocating
anarchy. But they nonetheless have had a significant im-
pact on the teaching of English in the schools. When
teachers refer to the "linguistic approach," they generally mean structural or descriptive linguistics.

States and Operations. But again we can note a pre-
occupation. Most of the followers of Sapir (and more particularly of Bloomfield) were so concerned with describing
the way language *is* that for a long time they ignored the
way language *operates*. That is, and somewhat more technically, they did not concern themselves with the distinction between **states** and **operations**. When a linguist or a
physicist refers to a "state" or a "static condition" of an
object, he wishes to "freeze" that object in an instant of
time. For example, a physicist might say that a light bulb
can be in two states: "on" or "off." He can then describe
these states very precisely. But in doing so, he says nothing
about how a light bulb gets from one state to another. There
is, of course, nothing wrong in describing states; on the
contrary, a physicist will probably draw upon such descriptions when he comes to describe operations. But it is
equally true that describing states may well be—and generally is—very different from describing operations. And
this difference underlies the distinction between descrip-

tive grammar, on the one hand, and transformational grammar, on the other.

A transformational grammar seeks to describe the operations of language. Naturally, in doing this it must also describe the various states of language. The current controversy in linguistics is largely concerned with the question of what is the best method of describing both states and operations. At this point in our explication, the question is inordinately technical and need not concern us. This text, in short, is a presentation of a pedagogical transformational grammar, rather than a justification of such a grammar relative to other kinds of grammars. Nonetheless, the question of the need for transformations in a generative grammar of English is important, and we will return to it from time to time in the discussion that follows. Taken together, these later references attempt to establish that, although transformations may not be necessary in a grammar of English, their use considerably simplifies such a grammar.

1.2   THE FUNCTION AND NATURE OF GRAMMAR

The various distinctions we have noted thus far raise another problem: what is the function of grammar? This, of course, is an extremely broad question which every generation of teachers would probably answer differently. At any time, the answer depends upon the available linguistic facts. At this time we can give at least two answers, both of which are valid. A grammar should somehow explain a native speaker's intuition about his language. A grammar should also be an aid in increasing a speaker's competence. These answers lead to a more fundamental question: what *is* a grammar? Again, this question is extremely broad. As we have already noted, linguists and psychologists have very little notion of how to characterize the "internal grammar" that an individual uses in producing or understanding sentences. Consequently, although we can answer the question by saying that a grammar "is a device that generates all of the grammatical sequences of [a language] and none of the ungrammatical ones,"[8] we have no idea of how to go about describing an individual's internal grammar. On the other hand, we can describe—at least in theory —a scientific grammar that performs the same functions as an internal grammar, and that is part of the task of this book.

The aim of transformationalists, then, is very different from that of the structuralists. Consequently, there is no need to assume that transformationalists are bound by the same restrictions. In particular, the transformationalists have no objections to relying on intuition in developing their theory; in fact, they insist that such reliance is a necessary prelude to the formulation of grammatical rules. In other words, the transformationalists are quite "traditional" in many of their aims. They have the advantage of two hundred years of scholarship which the eighteenth century English grammarians did not have. They can, and do, draw freely on the findings of the historical, comparative, and descriptive grammarians. They also have the tools of modern logic to draw upon, particularly those that relate to symbolic operations. They recognize, as their predecessors did not, that every language has its own logic and that Latin and Greek are neither more nor less logical than any other languages. In sum, they seek to describe, and more importantly, to explain a native speaker's intuition—or competence—with respect to his language.

1.3 THE OLD AND THE NEW

In one very important sense, then, transformational grammar is a new way of looking at some old and traditional ideas concerning language. It is neither esoteric nor forbidding in its aims. And if it seems so in its methods, it is only because we—that is, teachers and prospective teachers

---

[8] Noam Chomsky, *Syntactic Structures* ('s-Gravenhage, Mouton & Co., 1957), p. 13. Of course, only an ideal grammar will generate *all* of the grammatical sequences of a language.

of English—have not made use of all the devices that modern scholarship offers us. We have not recognized that Huxley's statement in defense of the theory of evolution —"Irrationally held truths may be more harmful than reasoned errors"—may apply to our attitudes toward grammar.

To the writer of this book, it seems that many teachers have not kept pace with modern scholarship. They have been content merely to preserve the traditional; they have not nurtured it and helped it grow. They have failed to continue what the eighteenth century grammarians began. They have provided a window to the past rather than a bridge from the past to the future. They—and we—must now reassess our obligations.

These obligations, of course, are creative. Transformational grammar is not complete. As we noted early in this chapter, the details of the grammar are changing now and will continue to change. We should, in fact, contribute to this change. All this means that the sections which follow are not a "grammar of English." Some of the details are undoubtedly wrong; others are needlessly complicated. Future grammarians will correct the former and improve the latter. But that is not our present concern. We have much to learn from our colleagues in the sciences. In particular, we must recognize that all theories are merely that: theories. They are subject to replacement by more comprehensive and powerful theories. But this fact does not prevent scientists from working out theories in detail. English is no less a living subject matter than physics and chemistry. And teachers of English have a definite obligation to theorize about their subject matter. They have an obligation to develop the details of grammatical theories and to test them against the reality of experience and intuition. They have an obligation to keep their subject alive. And in fulfilling their obligations, they must make use of all the information which scholars provide about their subject. In short, they have an obligation to teach "living English," and transformational grammar offers one theory of how English lives.

Discussion

1. What are some of the significant ways in which a pedagogical grammar differs from a scientific grammar? This text, of course, is a pedagogical grammar, written for teachers and prospective teachers of English. In what way or ways would it be different if it were written for students in the secondary schools? Consider some foreign language that you have studied and list some of the ways in which a pedagogical grammar designed to teach that language to a native speaker of English would be different from one designed to teach the same native speaker of English the principles of his own language.

2. Discuss some of the ways in which nonlinguistic factors affect linguistic performance. As teachers, we have generally been concerned with written performance or with the restricted spoken performance that occurs in the classroom. What are some other situations in which a student's performance might be a more accurate index of his competence? What does the distinction between competence and performance suggest about assigning grades for "grammar"? Discuss this thesis: the greater the self-confidence of a speaker, the more his performance will duplicate his competence.

3. Read one of the many popularizations of "modern logic" and then discuss the essential differences between modern and classical logic. Many of the weaknesses of *applied* traditional grammar (such as the grammatical rules found in textbooks) are due to the fact that such grammar is based on classical logic. What are some of these weaknesses and how are they related to the weaknesses inherent in classical logic? Discuss some of the advantages that have accrued to teachers of mathematics as a result of the application of modern logic to their field. What do these advantages suggest for teachers of English?

4. Compare a selection from Chaucer written in Middle

English with a modern "translation" of the same selection. Pay particular attention to spelling, word order, and inflectional endings. What are the significant differences between the two selections, and what relevance do these differences have for teachers of English?

5. What objections does Chomsky make to Skinner's book, *Verbal Behavior* (see footnote 4, p. 7)? What significance do these objections have for teachers of English? How does Chomsky propose that linguists — and psychologists — should overcome these objections?

6. Compare the word for *father*, and the words for the numbers *one, two*, and *three* in the languages listed in Table 1.1. Compare these same words with their earlier forms in Old and Middle English (as given, for example, in the *Oxford English Dictionary*). What similarities do you note? Can the words be grouped into subfamilies? What conclusions can you draw about language change?

7. Discuss this thesis: form underlies meaning. Give examples of situations in which a change of form radically affects meaning. List some of the "formal" properties of English. Compare these formal properties with those of some foreign language you have studied. What conclusions can you draw about the function of formal properties in language and about the relation of these properties to meaning?

8. Discuss Chomsky's definition of "grammar" (p. 15) and compare it with the definitions given in the *Oxford English Dictionary* and Merriam-Webster's *Third International Dictionary*. In what way or ways do school grammars (i.e., those used as texts in elementary and secondary schools and in colleges and universities) conform to Chomsky's definition? In what ways do they depart from the definition? What do these facts suggest about the difference between a scientific and a pedagogical grammar on the one hand, and between a traditional grammar and a modern grammar on the other?

9. Discuss the relationship between theory and practice in the teaching of English? Does the same relationship hold for the teaching of mathematics? biology? history? How much knowledge of theory should a teacher have? a student?

10. Some wit once said, "No one, not even a purist, seriously objects to the fact that language changes. Rather, what we object to is the people who change it." How true is this epigram? What examples can you find of language changes made by people? What arguments can you advance in favor of language change? against language change? How does language change affect the teacher? the linguist? the student?

⟨2⟩

The English Sentence

Observe how system into system runs.

POPE, *An Essay on Man.*

English, like every other natural language, is complex, flexible, changing, and systematic. The basis of this system is the sentence.

Before we look at the sentence, however, we must look briefly at the nature of language itself. We got some notion of the complexity of language previously when we examined the sentences:

Sentence 1.1 John is easy to please.
Sentence 1.2 John is eager to please.

But the complexity is actually much deeper. Take two more sentences that Chomsky has frequently used for illustration:

Sentence 2.1 I expected the doctor to examine John.
Sentence 2.2 I persuaded the doctor to examine John.

Superficially (that is, on the face or surface of language), these latter two sentences are quite similar. But note how they behave when we change them from the active to the passive voice:

Sentence 2.1a I expected John to be examined by the doctor.
Sentence 2.2a I persuaded John to be examined by the doctor.

21

In Sentence 2.1, the speaker expects that an event will happen, viz., that *the doctor will examine John*. When this sentence is changed from the active to the passive voice, the expectation remains much the same, for if *the doctor will examine John*, it is also true that *John will be examined by the doctor*. But a very different situation prevails with Sentence 2.2. In the case of the active voice, the speaker is persuading the *doctor*. And this is obviously quite different from the case of the corresponding sentence in the passive voice (Sentence 2.2a) where the speaker is persuading *John*.

In other words, although the original sentences appear, at first glance, to be similar – and actually are *on the surface* – every mature native speaker of English knows that they are somehow different. This fact has led linguists, and should lead us, to suspect that in addition to the **surface structure** of language there is also a **deep structure**. We will return to this important distinction frequently in the following chapters.[1]

Language is also extremely flexible. Take, for example, the difference between declarative and interrogative sentences. If we set out to design a language, we would certainly want to be able to ask questions in that language. But would we recognize the wide variety of possibilities available to us in asking questions? Suppose we have the sentence:

Sentence 2.3 My roommate was quietly eating sunflower seeds in class today.

---

[1] We could obviously say that the difference between the sentences is purely semantic. This is in some sense true, but it is not very revealing. In particular, it does not offer a logical explanation of why the passive voice forms of the sentences are different. Syntax and semantics touch in many places, but insofar as possible we want to remember our earlier statement that "form underlies meaning." That is, we want to make certain that differences in semantics do not conceal differences in syntax, since it is frequently these latter differences (assuming we can isolate them) that will help us to understand the semantic differences.

We can interrogate the subject, object, and verb:

Sentence 2.3a Who was eating sunflower seeds? (subject)
Sentence 2.3b What was my roommate eating? (object)
Sentence 2.3c What was my roommate doing in class today?
(verb)

We can also interrogate the adverbs of time, location, and manner:

Sentence 2.3d When was my roommate eating sunflower
seeds? (time)
Sentence 2.3e Where was my roommate eating sunflower
seeds? (location)
Sentence 2.3f How was my roommate eating sunflower
seeds? (manner)

These kinds of questions, as we will note later, can be called *wh-* questions since (with the obvious exception of the irregular form *how*) they all begin with one of the *wh-* words: *who, what, when, where.*

But we can also ask a variety of questions that can be answered with a "Yes" or "No." Sentence 2.3g is the so-called **regular yes/no question**. Sentences 2.3h and 2.3i are known as **tag questions**. And Sentence 2.3j, which has a rising inflection as if the person speaking were incredulous, is called an **echo question**.

Sentence 2.3g Was my roommate quietly eating sunflower
seeds in class today? (regular yes/no)
Sentence 2.3h My roommate was quietly eating sunflower
seeds in class today, wasn't she? (negative tag)
Sentence 2.3i My roommate wasn't quietly eating sunflower
seeds in class today, was she? (positive tag)
Sentence 2.3j My roommate was quietly eating sunflower
seeds in class today? (echo)

At this point, such flexibility is probably confusing, but we shall see in later chapters that it is quite systematic.

Language is constantly changing. We have already seen in Chapter 1 that Old English was primarily an inflected

language. During the past fifteen hundred years English
has been changing—and developing—in the direction of
fewer inflections and more rigid word order. But there are
also other obvious changes. As the more than two hundred
million people who speak and read English as either a native or foreign language know all too well, the spelling system of English is chaotic, at least on the surface. George
Bernard Shaw was fond of illustrating this chaos by citing
the word *ghoti* which, he claimed, was a perfectly reasonable way to spell the English word *fish*. The *gh-* has the
pronunciation found in the word *enough*; the *-o-* has the
pronunciation of *women*; and the *-ti* has the pronunciation of *action*. Several hundred years ago, when the spelling of words became fixed because of the demands of the
newly invented printing press, Shaw's example would not
have had much meaning because most English words
were pronounced exactly as we spell them (rather than
pronounce them) today. In short, the pronunciation of
English, as every student of Chaucer knows, has changed
radically throughout the centuries.

Word meanings have also changed. Words like *anon*
and *presently*, which now mean "in a little while," originally meant "immediately," "at this very instant." And
there is certainly no reason to suspect that language has
stopped changing. Languages are changed by people, generally because of the changing patterns of the societies in
which they live.

Above all, however, and almost in spite of the flexibility,
complexity, and changing nature of language, it remains
rigidly systematic. Language has rules. A grammar is,
among other things, a collection of these rules. Our knowledge of these rules permits us to understand and produce
sentences.

The English language is an infinite system. There are
more sentences in the language than can be counted, and
there is no "longest sentence" in the language. For example, we can say: "I saw one star" or "I saw two stars"
and so on up to infinity. We can also say: "That statement

is very silly" or "That statement is very, very silly," and we can keep adding another *very* to any sentence like this one. No one, that is, can make a list of all the sentences in English, and no one can point to the longest sentence.

In this respect, English is like mathematics. There are rules of sentence formation just as there are rules of multiplication. In arithmetic we learn one set of rules that tells us how to multiply all the numbers from one to ten by each other; we also learn a set of rules for applying the rules of the first set to numbers larger than ten. With these two sets of rules, we are able to multiply an infinite number of numbers. We can also use these rules to "check" (that is, in a sense, "to understand") someone else's multiplication. And this analogy suggests why linguists turn to symbolic logic (which is highly mathematical) when they are trying to formulate the rules of language.

2.1 LANGUAGE

In *Syntactic Structures*, Chomsky gives the following definition:

> [A language is] a set (finite or infinite) of sentences, each finite in length and constructed out of a finite set of elements.[2]

This important definition, which sums up much of what we have said to this point, requires some comment.

Chomsky is here talking about all languages, both natural and man-made (man-made languages would include, for example, those which are used in computing machines; they are vastly simpler than human—or natural—languages). Many man-made languages are finite; that is, the number of sentences in the language can be counted, and it is possible to "point to" the longest sentence. English and, to the best of the writer's knowledge, all other natural languages, are infinite.

---

[2] *Syntactic Structures*, p. 13.

The word **set**, as Footnote 5 in Chapter 1 indicates, is used in a technical sense. For our purposes, we can consider a set as a collection of anything. A set may contain an infinite number of things (such as, for example, the set of all possible integers in mathematics), or it may contain only one thing (such as the Eiffel Tower). When adapted to our purposes, then, the first part of the definition says that the English language is a set or collection of the infinite number of possible English sentences.

The second part of the definition says that there is no "infinitely long sentence." This is a very different thing from saying that there is no "longest sentence." If sentences were infinitely long, we could not possibly understand them. In other words, every sentence, by definition, must be finite in length, but it is always possible to make any one of these finite sentences at least one word longer.[3]

Finally, the definition says that every sentence is made up of elements, that we can collect these elements into a set, and that the number of elements can be counted. Some of these elements, for example, will be the letters of the alphabet (or more precisely, the sounds represented by the letters of some kind of phonetic alphabet); obviously, we need only a very limited number of these letters. Other elements will be words, and it is certainly possible to count all the words in an English dictionary. Still other elements will be grammatical relations such as the agreement between subject and verb in English. And all of these various things constitute a **set of elements**.

We can now rephrase the definition:

> The English language is made up of an infinite number of sentences. Every individual sentence, however, is finite in length. And every sentence is constructed from a relatively limited number of elements.

---

[3] Readers who lack the training in mathematics to appreciate this rather fine distinction should not be unduly alarmed. The distinction will certainly become more obvious in later chapters, particularly when we demonstrate how a grammar generates sentences.

This definition is worth noting for another reason. It defines "language" in terms of "sentences"; that is, it assumes that the reader knows, perhaps intuitively, what a sentence is. Our earlier definition of a grammar (given in Chapter 1) as "a device that generates all of the grammatical sequences of [a language] and none of the ungrammatical ones," makes a similar assumption since sentences are obviously "grammatical sequences." Most of our later definitions will also assume a knowledge of sentences. This fact is undoubtedly disconcerting to many readers, particularly those who have come to rely on the "definitions" of traditional grammar. We should, therefore, pause to consider the theoretical questions which such usage raises.

Again, we can usefully draw an analogy. As Robert B. Lees has pointed out in discussing this same problem, the "working biologist" very rarely, "if ever," attempts to define the notion of "cell," although this notion "underlies all of biology." He goes on to point out that there is no procedure whereby a biologist can determine whether a given object "is a cell or is not a cell."

> This requirement is not necessary in order to use intelligently the notion *cell* or for that matter in order to intelligently explicate the notion *cell*, and similarly to explicate notions on the *basis* of the notion *cell*, for example tissue, or bone.

And he concludes by noting that if we "already knew how to define 'grammatical sentence of English,' there would be no earthly reason for trying to formulate a theory of English sentences, i.e., an English grammar."[4]

Lees is saying, in effect, that the only valid definition of "grammatical sentence in English" is a complete grammar

---

[4] Robert B. Lees, "Discussion," in *Report on the Eleventh Annual Round Table Meeting on Linguistics and Language Studies*, Bernard Choseed, ed. (Washington, D. C., Georgetown University Press, 1962), pp. 52, 181–182.

of English. He is also saying that no other discipline, including mathematics, physics, and chemistry, even makes a pretense of defining its basic elements *except in terms of each other*. Thus, we cannot define the axioms of Euclidean geometry, but we can use these axioms to develop theorems. Using Einstein's theory, we can define space and time in terms of each other, but we cannot define them outside of the system which the physicist uses to investigate the universe. We can, as the chemist does, define oxygen as that element which combines with two parts of hydrogen to give water, but this is really a circular definition because we also say that water is that compound which is made up of two parts hydrogen and one part oxygen.

Lees' point relates to the point that was made at the end of the last chapter. In the twentieth century, all of the major academic disciplines—except English—have abandoned the notion that precise and absolute definition is possible. They have, in short, developed earlier traditions in the light of contemporary advances. Many teachers of English have failed to develop their tradition. And this failure has placed tremendous—perhaps impossible—burdens on them.

But what about the old traditional definition: "A sentence is a group of words containing a subject and predicate and expressing a complete thought." (Many current school grammars omit the phrase "containing a subject and predicate," but this omission neither improves nor weakens the definition.) The definition, of course, is semantic; that is, it assumes that the reader knows the *meaning* of the phrase "a complete thought." Certainly this notion has defied philosophers for thousands of years. Plato wrote an entire book, *The Republic*, trying to define not a complete thought but a single word: *justice*. Even that attempt was not successful. The conclusion is inescapable, and schoolchildren have known it for years. The definition is meaningless unless we know already what a sentence is.

Actually, the lack of notional definition of sentence will not in any way hinder the presentation of a transformational grammar of English. We shall, in fact, find the presentation simpler, more meaningful, and more revealing because we are no longer "hot for certainties" which, at this stage of our understanding, are beyond our grasp.

2.2   BASIC ENGLISH SENTENCES

The simplest place to begin our discussion of English grammar is with the notion of basic English sentences. And the most elemental description of a basic sentence divides the sentence into two parts: a **subject** and **predicate**. This fact, of course, was also obvious to the older traditional grammarians and indicates again the close tie between traditional and transformational grammar.

For purposes of elaboration, particularly later in the text when we discuss such things as subordination, it is convenient to represent some of these descriptions symbolically. Such representation also helps to insure accuracy, since it frequently makes errors in description more obvious. Consequently, we shall adopt the following symbols:

Sentence: S
Noun Phrase: NP
Verb Phrase: VP

Thus, we may say that a **sentence** (S) consists of a subject, which is a **noun phrase** (NP), plus a predicate, which is a **verb phrase** (VP). Or, more succinctly:[5]

PS 2.1 $S \longrightarrow NP + VP$

where the arrow means "may be rewritten." This formula is not a definition of "sentence" since we do not know precisely what a "noun phrase" and "verb phrase" are. On the other hand, the formula does define two grammatical re-

---

[5] Other symbols and rules are presented throughout the text. The PS number in front of the rule is similar to the sentence number. It designates a "phrase-structure" rule, and these rules are numbered consecutively throughout each chapter.

lationships. That is, we may say that a "subject" is the *NP* of *S*, and a "predicate" is the *VP* of *S*.

On this elemental level, all this may be so obvious that to dwell upon the fact seems ridiculous. But the relationships will become more complex as the grammar unfolds. And consequently, it is worth the time at this point to be certain that we understand precisely what these obvious facts mean. We may, therefore, sum up this brief presentation:

1. A sentence (*S*) consists of a noun phrase (*NP*) and a verb phrase (*VP*).
2. The "subject" of a sentence, by definition, is the *NP* of *S*; the "predicate" of a sentence, also by definition, is the *VP* of *S*.
3. The terms "subject" and "predicate" express grammatical relationships.

We may also express this information graphically in a **branching tree diagram**. These "trees" are similar to the diagraming of traditional grammar, but there is one extremely important difference. In particular, "branching trees" are unique; that is, given a sentence which is not structurally ambiguous, there is *one and only one way* of representing it with this system. As even a cursory check of several school grammars will indicate, there is wide disagreement among authors concerning the "rules" of traditional diagraming; such disagreement is impossible in transformational grammar.[6] As was the case with our symbolic presentation, the tree probably seems inordinately

---

[6] Once, while teaching a course called "English Grammar for Teachers," the writer assigned several apparently simple sentences for diagraming. The students were told to consult two or three different textbooks currently being used in high schools in the Middle West. In most cases, the students found three or four different ways of diagraming a single sentence. In one case ("I told him to take the book back."), they found seven ways; in another ("We asked for whoever might be there."), they found eight; and in one spectacular case ("He was older than his brother."), they found a total of ten different ways. The rules for making branching tree diagrams were designed, in part, to overcome this ambiguity.

simple at this point and no doubt is; the trees, however, will become more complicated later. The dots in the tree are called **nodes**. The "S node" is said to **dominate** the "*NP* node" and the "*VP* node." The lines connecting the nodes are, quite naturally, called **branches**.

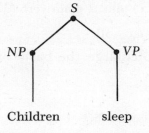

Figure 2.1   S ⟶ NP + VP.

We run into complexity at the very next step in elaborating a pedagogical grammar of English sentences. In particular, we must decide how to handle the verb *to be*. There is little doubt that *to be* is different from all other verbs in English. For example, if we look at all the so-called regular verbs in English, we find that—excluding auxiliaries—each one has only *four* distinct forms:

    call, calls, called, calling
    walk, walks, walked, walking

None of the so-called irregular verbs (except the verb *to be*) has more than five distinct forms:

    hit, hits, hitting
    sing, sings, sang, sung, singing

On the other hand, *to be* has *eight* distinct forms:

    be, is, am, are, was, were, been, being

There are sound historical reasons for this variety, just as there are also historical reasons for the fact that *to be* behaves differently in sentences from all other verbs. And for these reasons, among others, it is simplest and most convenient to divide the verbs initially into two categories: (1) *to be* and (2) all other verbs.

Yet all "main verbs"—including the verb *to be*—can be preceded by auxiliaries. Thus, our next symbolic presentation says that a verb phrase (*VP*) may consist of one or more **auxiliary verbs** (*Aux*) plus a **main verb** (*MV*):

PS 2.2 $VP \longrightarrow Aux + MV$

Now, we can also enlarge the basic branching tree diagram:

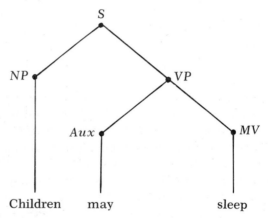

Figure 2.2   NP + Aux + MV.

And we can make the notion of "dominate" more specific. In particular, we may say that *VP* "immediately dominates" *Aux* and *MV*; *S* "immediately dominates" *NP* and *VP*; and *S* simply "dominates" *Aux* and *MV*. In other words, one node "immediately dominates" the next node down the branch and only "dominates" any node further down the branch.

We can now treat the distinction between *to be* and all other verbs. In particular, we say that a main verb consists of *either* the verb *to be* followed by a predicate complement *or* any other verb. Symbolically, we may state this as follows:

PS 2.3 $\quad MV \longrightarrow \left\{ \begin{array}{c} be + Pred \\ V \end{array} \right\}$

The braces—{ }—indicate a choice. That is, when we come to the *MV* node in a branching tree, we may choose either *be* + *Pred* or *V*. Thus, the simple rules we have given thus far permit us to derive two branching trees:

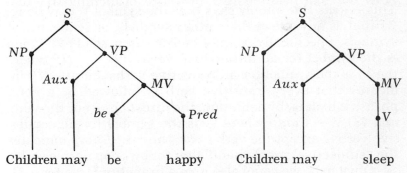

Figure 2.3 Expanding MV.

At this point, it is useful to oversimplify somewhat in order to make the presentation more clear. The oversimplification is not serious, and we shall correct it in a subsequent chapter before developing this aspect of transformational theory further. In particular, we want to say now that there are three primary types of verb (V) in English: **intransitive** (V_i), **transitive** (V_t), and **copulative** (V_c).[7] Any verb in English may be followed by an adverb of location or time (or both). With intransitive verbs, however, nothing intervenes between the verb and the adverb. With transitive verbs, a direct object (and sometimes an indirect ob-

---

[7] In this presentation, the copulative verb (V_c) excludes the verb *to be*, but includes most of the verbs traditionally called **linking verbs**, e.g., *seem, become, taste,* and so on.

ject) intervenes between the verb and the adverb. With
copulative verbs, the so-called subjective complement intervenes; as we shall note more fully later, the kinds of
words that can occur as subjective complements are sometimes different from those than can occur as predicates
following the verb *to be*.

Again, all this can be shown graphically:

$$\text{PS 2.4} \quad V \longrightarrow \begin{Bmatrix} V_i \\ V_t + NP \\ V_c + Comp \end{Bmatrix}$$

This **rewrite rule** simply says that the symbol V may be rewritten as any one of three other symbols, or sequences of
symbols. Specifically, V may be rewritten as (1) V_i which
is the symbol for all intransitive verbs, (2) $V_t + NP$ where
the V_t is the symbol for all transitive verbs and the NP indicates that every transitive verb is followed by a noun
phrase which is, by definition, the direct object of the verb,
and (3) $V_c + Comp$ where V_c is the symbol for all copulative verbs — except the verb *to be* — and the $Comp$ indicates
the "subjective complement" that follows copulative verbs.

Obviously, we could also give a branching tree for each
of the alternatives indicated in this formula. One possible
tree is shown on the facing page; the reader may wish to
draw his own trees for the other possibilities. We should
notice, here, that a second NP has been introduced into
our branching tree. This NP is not a "subject" because it
is not immediately dominated by S. Rather, we may define
this NP as the **direct object** because it is immediately dominated by a V node which also immediately dominates a
V_t node. This description is therefore a specification of the
intimate connection between transitive verbs and direct
objects; it also indicates that other kinds of verbs cannot
have direct objects.

Before developing additional facts about the language,
it is profitable to pause at this elementary stage and sum
up the facts presented thus far. At the same time, we can
introduce another important notion which we have tacitly
assumed in the earlier part of this chapter: sentence posi-

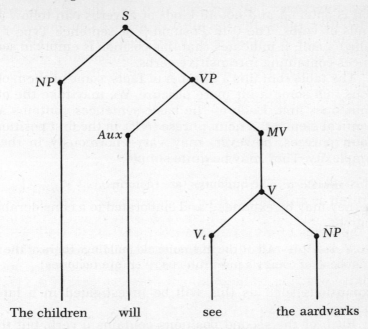

Figure 2.4 NP + Aux + V$_t$ + NP.

tions. The following table gives the basic sentence types in English, and arranges the elements in these sentences according to positions:

Type	Position			
	1	2	3	4
to be	NP	*be*	*Pred*	(*Adv*)
I	NP	V$_i$	∅	(*Adv*)
II	NP	V$_t$	NP	(*Adv*)
III	NP	V$_c$	*Comp*	(*Adv*)

Table 2.1 Basic Sentence Positions

As the table indicates, there are four basic positions in simple English sentences; the fourth, or adverbial, position is optional and not all kinds of adverbs can follow all kinds of verbs. The $\emptyset$ in Position 3 of sentence Type I is called a **null**; it indicates that this position is empty in sentences containing intransitive verbs.

The table contains a number of facts, some of them obvious and some a bit more obscure. We may take the obvious ones first. Each of the basic sentences contains an identical element, a noun phrase (*NP*), in the first position. Noun phrases, however, may vary enormously in their complexity. They may be quite simple:

Sentence 2.4a   The buildings (are factories).

Or they may be expanded and elaborated to a considerable degree:

Sentence 2.4b   All of the five quite old buildings there at the bend of county's most famous river (are factories).

Expansions such as this will be investigated in a later chapter.

Each of the second positions contains a verb, but the verb obviously differs according to the type of sentence. Most of the verbs in English can be assigned easily to one of the major categories, but there are a few verbs that do not fit the categories perfectly. These latter verbs we shall treat in restricted categories. On the other hand, the particular kind of verb is a good indicator of sentence type, and, consequently, we may say that the nature of the verb defines the sentence type.

The third position contains the greatest variety. Following the verb *to be* we have an element known as a predicate (*Pred*). The predicate can be a noun phrase (*The boy is my brother*), an adjective (*The boy is tall*), or an adverb of location (*The boy is here*). Symbolically, this is shown as follows:

$$PS\ 2.5 \quad Pred \longrightarrow \begin{Bmatrix} NP \\ Adj \\ Loc \end{Bmatrix}$$

Following intransitive verbs, the third position is empty. This description may seem artificial at this point, but in an over-all analysis of English, the description is clearly preferable, since it makes the comments on the fourth—or adverbial—position more inclusive and general. The *NP* which follows transitive verbs in the basic sentence patterns is also known as the direct object. We have already indicated that the subjective complement which follows copulative verbs is different in significant ways from the predicate (*Pred*) which follows the verb *to be*.

As the parentheses in Table 2.1 indicate, the fourth position is optional. Yet adverbs are so basic to the language, and occur with such frequency, that the simplest pedagogical description of English is one which includes them as part of the structure of basic sentences. We should note, however, that the symbol for **adverb** (*Adv*) is generalized at this point; certain restrictions on the use of adverbs will be discussed in later chapters. By way of preview, we may note that *to be* can be followed in the fourth position by **adverbs of location** (*Loc*) and **adverbs of time** (*Tm*) but not by **adverbs of manner** (*Man*). That is, we can say *John is happy there* and *John is happy today*, but we cannot say **John is happy furiously*.

There are in English many sentences which apparently do not conform to these basic patterns. For example, the sentence *Come here!* appears not to contain an *NP* in Position 1, and the sentence *We elected John president today* appears to contain two noun phrases in Position 3. These irregularities are apparent rather than real, however, and can be dealt with quite logically once we have established the notion of basic sentence types.

The sentence types given in Table 2.1 are those forms which underlie all **kernel sentences**. (However, we also want to include the auxiliary verbs in the notion of kernel sentences.) All other sentences in English are **nonkernel** or, to use a more descriptive term, **derived sentences**. The kernel sentences form the backbone of the language; all other sentences can be derived from them through various operations.[8] In deriving sentences, we first select one or more **nonkernel options** (e.g., "interrogative" and "passive") and then we perform various transformations upon the elements in the sentence to produce a nonkernel sentence.

The following are examples of the kernel sentence types given in Table 2.1:

to be	Sentence 2.5	The animal is an aardvark.
	Sentence 2.6	The aardvark may be happy.
	Sentence 2.7	The aardvark has been there.
Type I:	Sentence 2.8	The forest is sleeping.
	Sentence 2.9	The dew has fallen.
	Sentence 2.10	The parachutist may jump tomorrow.
Type II:	Sentence 2.11	The Frenchman drank the wine yesterday.
	Sentence 2.12	The draftsman may have bought an elephant.
	Sentence 2.13	The aardvark is eating his supper.
Type III:	Sentence 2.14	The professor has become angry.
	Sentence 2.15	The team looks terrible today.
	Sentence 2.16	The steak tastes good.

All of these kernel sentences may be represented by branching trees, as shown on the facing page (the trees are somewhat simplified).

2.3 FIRST MODEL GRAMMAR

We can now give a vastly simplified **model grammar** that will generate kernel sentences. The grammar will be enlarged considerably as we work through a more realistic presentation of English, and most importantly, we shall introduce the notion of transformations. But the fundamental principles that underlie the grammar will not change.

---

[8] More precisely, as we shall see, nonkernel sentences are derived from the structures which underlie kernel sentences.

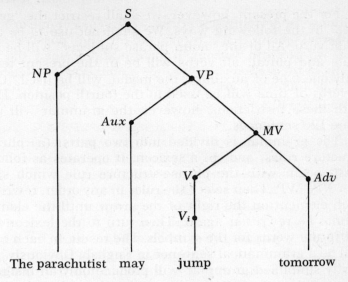

Figure 2.5   Sentence 2.10.

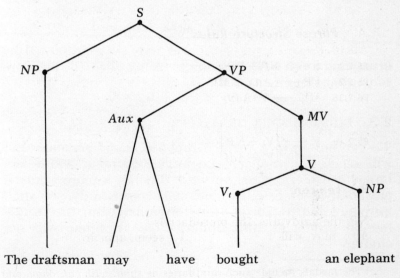

Figure 2.6   Sentence 2.12.

For the present, however, we shall restrict the "grammar" in the following ways. We shall not use *to be* as a main verb. All of the "noun phrase subjects" will be animate and plural; all verbs will be in the present tense. Only one type of auxiliary, the modal, will be used.[9] Only adverbs of time will be used in the fourth position. Even with these restrictions, however, the grammar will generate 120 sentences.

The grammar is divided into two parts: (a) phrase-structure rules, and (b) a lexicon. It operates as follows. First, begin with the phrase-structure rule which says: $S \rightarrow NP + VP$. Then select the rules in any order, rewriting each element on the right of the arrow until the element cannot be rewritten again. Then turn to the lexicon and substitute words for the symbols. The result, in each case, will be a grammatical sentence in English. Obviously, this vastly simplified grammar will produce only an insignificant number of sentences, but each sentence produced by the grammar will be grammatical. Each sentence can also be represented by a unique branching tree diagram.

A. Phrase-Structure Rules[10]

PS 2.1 $S \longrightarrow NP + VP$
PS 2.2 $VP \longrightarrow Aux + MV$
PS 2.3a $MV \longrightarrow V\ (Adv)$

PS 2.4a $V \longrightarrow \begin{Bmatrix} V_i \\ V_t + NP \\ V_c + Adj \end{Bmatrix}$

B. Lexicon

NP: the aardvarks, the pterodactyls
Aux: may, will V_c: seem, appear

---

[9] The modals include such auxiliaries as *shall, will, can, may*, and so on.

[10] Notice that rules PS 2.3a and PS 2.4a are simplified forms of rules presented earlier in the chapter.

V_i: dance, run   *Adj*: lonesome, hungry
V_t: see, devour   *Adv*: today, tomorrow

The symbols have the following meanings: the arrow ($\longrightarrow$) means "rewrite as"; the braces—{ }—indicate that one complete line, and only one line, of the elements included within the braces must be chosen; the parentheses (around the *Adv* in rule PS 2.3a) indicate that the element contained within the parentheses is optional—a grammatical sentence will result whether or not the element is chosen.

The process of producing a sentence with this grammar is called a **derivation**. The following is a typical derivation:

   S
1. $NP + VP$ (using rule PS 2.1)
2. $NP + Aux + MV$ (rule PS 2.2)
3. $NP + Aux + V + Adv$ (rule PS 2.3a)
4. $NP + Aux + V_t + NP + Adv$ (rule PS 2.4a)

Then we substitute appropriate words from the lexicon to produce, for example:

Sentence 2.17   The aardvarks may see the pterodactyls today.

Or:

Sentence 2.18   The pterodactyls will devour the aardvarks tomorrow.

Notice that we "rewrite" only one item at a time. Thus, in going from step 1 to step 2 of the derivation, we rewrote *VP* as $Aux + MV$, and in going from step 3 to step 4, we rewrote *V* as $V_t + NP$. The restriction, that in phrase-structure rules we may rewrite only one element at a time, is an important part of all transformational grammars. It is this restriction which gives us a unique branching tree diagram for every derivation (see Figure 2.7 on page 42).

Another derivation from this simple set of rules might look quite different:

   S
1. $NP + VP$ (PS 2.1)

2. $NP + Aux + MV$ (PS 2.2)
3. $NP + Aux + V$ (PS 2.3a)
4. $NP + Aux + V_i$ (PS 2.4a)

This is as far as the phrase-structure rules will take us. The final line of this derivation (i.e., $NP + Aux + V_i$) is known as a **terminal string**; we might say that the elements are "strung together" by the plus signs. But we also use the term **string** even if there are no plus signs in the line. Thus the "S" is called the **initial string**. Lines 1, 2, and 3 are called **intermediate strings**.

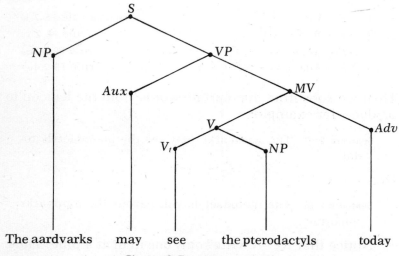

The aardvarks   may   see   the pterodactyls   today

Figure 2.7   Sentence 2.17.

When we come to the terminal string of the phrase-structure derivation, we substitute words from the lexicon for the symbols in the string:

Sentence 2.19   The aardvarks may dance.

Or:

Sentence 2.20   The pterodactyls will run.

Since both of these sentences have the same underlying derivation, they both have the same unique branching tree diagram. In other words, a branching tree diagram is merely a graphic means of presenting a derivation.[11] Two sentences can be represented with the same branching tree diagram if, and only if, their derivations in terms of phrase-structure rules are equivalent; that is, if their initial and terminal strings are identical.

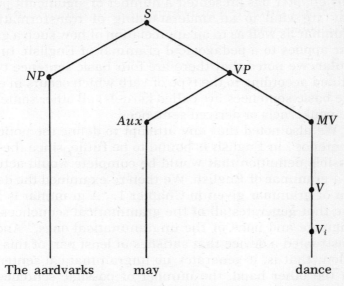

Figure 2.8   Sentence 2.19.

At least one advantage of a branching tree diagram over traditional diagraming can be seen in these examples:

_____

[11] Because the branching tree diagrams do represent the derivation of a string from phrase-structure rules, transformational grammarians occasionally refer to them as **phrase-structure markers**, or more briefly as P markers. The term **derivation**, which refers to the steps that lead from the initial string to the terminal string, should not be confused with the term, **derived**, which refers to a sentence or word which is made from another sentence or word (as, for example, *manly* is made from—or derived from—*man*).

each element is clearly labeled as a member of a particular category. Of all grammars available, only a transformational grammar can invariably provide a correct labeling of all elements while, at the same time, also showing grammatical relationships.

2.4 SUMMARY

This chapter has presented a number of significant points that are vital to an understanding of transformational grammar as well as to an appreciation of how such a grammar applies to a pedagogical grammar of English. In particular, we noted that there are four basic sentence types, defined according to the type of verb which occurs in each. The basic sentences are called kernels; all other sentences are nonkernels or derived sentences.

We also noted that any attempt to define the notion of "sentence" in English is bound to be futile, since the only possible definition that would be complete would actually be a grammar of English. We then re-examined the definition of grammar given in Chapter 1: "A grammar is a device that generates all of the grammatical sequences of a language and none of the ungrammatical ones." And we constructed a device that satisfies at least part of this definition; that is, it generates no ungrammatical sentences. On the other hand, the number of possible sentences in English is infinite, and our simplified grammar generates far less than a thousand sentences. Yet the principles that underlie an actual grammar of English are similar in many ways to those found in the simplified grammar. These principles will be the subject of several chapters that follow.

Discussion

1. Check some additional etymologies in the *Oxford English Dictionary* to see how words have changed in *meaning* over a period of time. In particular, check to see what

relationship exists between the two words *grammar* and *glamour* and to see what changes have taken place in such words as *nice* and *fond*. Discuss the implications of the fact that all languages change.

2. Technically speaking, a language can be infinite only if it has **recursive** rules (and these are discussed more fully in Chapter 4, Section 4.3). One rule introduces the word *very* (or *quite*) in front of descriptive adjectives, as the example in the text indicates. What are some of the other recursive elements in English? Can you think of other languages that have similar or identical recursive elements? How do the recursive elements of English (a "natural" language) compare with those of various mathematical languages such as arithmetic or algebra (which are "man-made" or "artificial")?

3. Discuss some examples (similar to Lees' example of biology and the impossibility of defining *cell*) which support the claim that the other major academic disciplines have abandoned the notion of precise definition in their discussion of fundamentals. Transformationalists generally feel that, although students may have a difficult time *labeling* such things as nouns and verbs in a sentence, they nonetheless know *intuitively* what these words are because they generally use them correctly in sentences. That is, to use Plato's terms, they have a knowledge "of" their language, but not a knowledge "about" their language. Discuss some of the implications of this belief. Can you think of any other areas where many people have a knowledge "of" – but not a knowledge "about" – something? For example, everyone knows how to tie a shoelace, but can you *explain* how to tie a shoelace using words only (no gestures, no pictures)?

4. As indicated in the text, the school-grammar definition of sentence is semantic and, for all practical purposes, meaningless if we do not know how to define "a complete thought" (something which no philosopher has ever been able to define). The school-grammar definitions of noun and verb are also semantic. To use them, in most cases, we must know what "names" and "actions" are. And, of course, if we already know what these words mean, we have no need for the definitions. Students use thousands of nouns and verbs correctly every day, but many of them have a difficult time *labeling* the nouns and verbs in a sentence. Discuss the usefulness, in a pedagogical grammar, of such labeling. What, precisely, do we expect a student to do with a definition? Are definitions more important in studying one's language or in studying a foreign language? Why?

5. Repeat the experiment, discussed in Footnote 6 (p. 30), of consulting several school grammars and applying the diagraming rules in these grammars to the following sentences:

> You don't have to worry about him.
> It is somehow personal and reassuring to save a dollar now
>   and then.
> Some of you young ladies may find this hard to believe.

What are some of the implications of the fact that each of these sentences can be diagramed in several ways? If the purpose of diagraming is to reveal structure to students, what are some of the disadvantages of having several different systems of diagraming that apparently reveal several different structures for the same sentence?

Exercises

1. Construct five kernel sentences for each of the basic sentence types given in Table 2.1. Use Sentences 2.5 to 2.16 as models.

2. Derive five sentences using the phrase-structure rules and the lexicon of the model grammar.

3. Draw branching tree diagrams for each of the derived sentences.

4. Identify the phrase-structure rules that are applied in the following derivation:

S

a. $NP + VP$ (PS 2.)
b. $NP + Aux + MV$ (PS 2.)
c. $NP + Aux + V$ (PS 2.)
d. $NP + Aux + V_c + Adj$ (PS 2.)

5. Complete the labeling of the nodes in the following branching tree diagram:

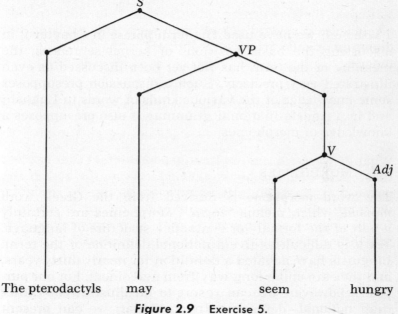

Figure 2.9 Exercise 5.

Words and Morphemes

Whate'er you think, good words, I think, were best.

SHAKESPEARE, *King John*, IV. iii. 28

Although we have used the term **phrase** in Chapter 2 in discussing the basic positions of kernel sentences, the meaning of the term has not yet been discussed or even illustrated very precisely. Such a discussion presupposes some knowledge of the various kinds of words in English; and in a transformational grammar, it also presupposes a knowledge of morphemes.

3.1 MORPHEMES

The word **morpheme** is derived from the Greek word *morphē* which means "form." Morphemes are certainly a part of the formal — or syntactic — structure of language. Yet it is difficult to give a notional definition of the term. Linguists have debated a definition for nearly thirty years, and they are still a long way from agreement. For our purposes, however, we can resort to an illustrative — rather than notional — definition. In particular, we can present several examples of English morphemes, and on the basis of these examples the reader can construct his own "working definition" of the term.

We know that languages are generally made up of individual words, which grammarians classify under the heading of "parts of speech." But not all parts of speech are complete words. In English, and in most other languages, there are in fact some parts of speech that are not complete words but that nonetheless occur again and again throughout the language. For example, there are many common affixes (i.e., prefixes and suffixes) in English:

> *un-   pre-   re-   -ly   -ness   -ish*

In addition, there is a small class of suffixes known as **inflectional endings**; the following are the most important:

-s, -es	indicating plurality in most nouns
-'s, -s'	indicating the genitive case in most nouns
-s, -es	indicating the third person singular, present tense of most verbs
-ed	indicating either the past tense or the past participle of many verbs
-ing	indicating the gerund or present participle forms of verbs
-er, -est	indicating, respectively, the comparative and superlative degrees of many adjectives.

All these affixes belong to a large class of items known as morphemes. In writing, linguists sometimes enclose morphemes within braces:

> {*un-*}   {*pre-*}   {*-ly*}   {*-ness*}   {*-s*}   {*-ed*}

But the category of morphemes contains other things in addition to affixes. As we have just noted, there is an {*-s*} morpheme on many nouns in English which serves the syntactic function of indicating plurality. Yet the feature of plurality may also be indicated in other ways; for example, by an *-es* (as in *dresses*), by an *-en* (as in *oxen*), by changing the vowel in the middle of the word (as in the change from *man* to *men*), and sometimes by nothing at all (as in *sheep* which can be either singular or plural).

In order to have a convenient means of discussing these various ways of indicating the feature of plurality, linguists use the term **plural morpheme** which, by definition, is the element that, when added to the singular form of a noun, changes that noun into the plural form, whatever it may be.

And there are other morphemes similar to the plural morpheme. For example, in discussing verbs linguists frequently speak of the **past participle morpheme** which is the element that, when added to the base form of the verb, produces the past participle form, whatever it may be. With regular verbs, the past participle morpheme takes the form of an *-ed* added to the verb base. If we add the past participle morpheme to the regular verb *walk* we produce *walked*. If, on the other hand, we add the past participle morpheme to such irregular verbs as *eat* and *drive*, then we produce the forms *eaten* and *driven*. And if we add the past participle morpheme to verbs like *sing* and *swim*, then we produce *sung* and *swum*.

[handwritten margin note: also called irregular . . strong verbs]

The following is a list of the symbols generally employed by transformational grammarians to indicate certain morphemes:

$\{Z_1\}$ the **agreement morpheme** that is generally indicated by the inflectional ending *-s* on the third person singular, present tense, of verbs (the subscript "1" differentiates this morpheme from the one that indicates plurality in nouns)

$\{-en\}$ the **past participle morpheme**

$\{Pas\}$ the **past tense morpheme**

$\{-ing\}$ the **present participle morpheme**

$\{Z_2\}$ the **plural morpheme**

$\{Z_3\}$ the **genitive morpheme**

These, then, are generalized morphemes. It is sometimes useful, however, to indicate the particular form that any generalized morpheme may take in a given instance. For example, the plural morpheme $\{Z_2\}$ may take any of the following forms in a particular word:

$\{-s\}$ $\{-es\}$ $\{-en\}$ $-\emptyset$

[handwritten margin note: or others]

(The $\emptyset$ is called a **zero morph**.) These varieties of the plural morpheme are known technically as **allomorphs**.

But morphemes are more than affixes. In fact, every word in English contains at least one morpheme. That is, *boy* might be considered as "boy" + ∅

individual words like *boy* and *walk* are morphemes, and
suffixes like *-s* and *-ed* are also morphemes. A word such
as *boys*, therefore, contains *two* morphemes: {*boy*}, which
can also stand alone and is therefore called a **free morpheme**; and {*-s*}, which must be joined to a word and is
therefore called a **bound morpheme**. In a word such as
walked, there are also two morphemes: {*walk*}, a free morpheme; and {*-ed*}, a bound morpheme. And in a word such
as *childishly*, there are three morphemes: {*child*}, a free
morpheme; {*-ish-*}, a bound morpheme; and {*-ly*}, another
bound morpheme.

We can sum up these initial illustrations by looking at
a word which contains five morphemes: *ungentlemanli-
ness*. The following morphemes are included:

1. the negative prefix morpheme {*un-*}, a bound morpheme
2. a free morpheme {*gentle*}
3. a second free morpheme {*man*}
4. a second bound morpheme {*-li-*}, which is an allomorph
   of the morpheme {*-ly*}
5. a third bound morpheme {*-ness*}, which can be called
   a **nominalization morpheme**

Finally, at least for this introductory discussion, we
must note that not all morphemes are indicated by particular sounds or varieties of spelling. We have, in fact,
already noted the existence of a zero morph which is an
allomorph of {Z_2} and occurs with such words as *sheep* and
moose. But there are also other kinds of morphemes that
are not indicated in a sentence by variations in spelling.
There is a difference, for example, between the following
sentences:

Sentence 3.1a   John has eaten the snails.
Sentence 3.1b   John *has* eaten the snails.

The second sentence is more emphatic, and we indicate
this difference—in print—with italics and—in speech—by
a combination of heavy accent and rising inflection on the
auxiliary verb. We can also say that the second sentence

contains the **emphatic morpheme** (sometimes also called the **affirmative morpheme**). The morpheme is indicated symbolically by $\{Emph\}$.

The **interrogative morpheme** is similar to the emphatic morpheme, since it is not always indicated in a sentence by a variation in spelling and sometimes not even by a variation in word order. Thus, we can have the question:

Sentence 3.2a   Has John eaten the snails?

which is called a yes/no question because it requires a "Yes" or "No" answer. But we can also have a variant of the yes/no question, called an echo question, by taking a simple statement and making the voice rise at the end:

Sentence 3.2b   John has eaten the snails?

And we can ask what linguists call a tag question:

Sentence 3.2c   John has eaten the snails, hasn't he?

The symbolic representation of each of these questions contains an interrogative morpheme, generally represented by $\{Q\}$.

All of this, perhaps, is rather a lot to digest at this point, and the reader may wish to turn to the first two exercises given at the end of this chapter. They are intended to reinforce the notion of morpheme given thus far. A greater understanding of morphemes in English will probably only come as a result of working sequentially through the following chapters. We may, however, sum up the major points concerning morphemes both by way of review and for convenience of reference:

1. Morphemes are regularly recurring features of English.
2. Every word contains at least one morpheme and may contain several.
3. There are two kinds of morphemes: bound and free.[1]

---

[1] Not all English words contain a free morpheme. Some, like *conceive, deceive, perceive*, and *receive*, are made up of two bound morphemes.

4. A basic morpheme, such as the plural morpheme, may
   be represented in spelling or pronunciation in more than
   one way; these variant ways are called allomorphs of
   the basic morpheme.

3.2 FORM WORDS AND STRUCTURE WORDS

The distinction between free and bound morphemes is
related to another distinction which linguists make: that
between **form words** and **structure words**.

Metaphorically, we can compare form and structure
words to bricks and mortar. The form words, which include
nouns, verbs, adjectives, and adverbs, provide the substance of an English sentence. The structure words, which
include auxiliary verbs, prepositions, and conjunctions,
serve primarily to give order to the substance; that is, they
hold the form words together in a meaningful sequence.

This distinction should not suggest that there is no difference in meaning between:

Sentence 3.3a   The boy hit the ball

and

Sentence 3.3b   The boy was hit by the ball

even though the only difference between the two sentences
is the addition of two structure words (*was, by*) in the second sentence.[2] Rather, the distinction should suggest that
the *primary* meaning in each sentence lies in the words
boy and *hit* and *ball*, and that the sentences would have *no*
meaning unless words such as these were included. For
example, there is certainly some meaning in the string of
words:

boy   hit   ball

---

[2] That is, this is the only *surface* difference. As we shall see subse-
quently, the branching tree diagram for the second sentence would contain the passive voice morpheme. The diagram would also indicate that
hit in the first sentence is the simple past tense, whereas in the second
sentence, it is the past participle.

But there is almost no meaning in the following string:

— the　was　by　the

The words *boy*, *hit*, and *ball* can also be inflected and can carry various derivational affixes. To put the matter another way, we can generally add some kind of bound morpheme to a form word. On the other hand, structure words generally cannot be inflected; that is, we cannot add bound morphemes to most structure words. The following words, which either contain bound morphemes or could have bound morphemes added to them, are all form words:

boy,　tall,　looked,　run,　goodness,　impossible,　quick

Thus *boy* can take the plural morpheme $\{-Z_2\}$, as well as such things as the adjectivalization morpheme: $\{-ish\}$. The adjectives *tall* and *quick* can both take the **comparative morpheme** $\{-er\}$, as well as the **superlative morpheme** $\{-est\}$; *quick* can also take the **adverbial morpheme** $\{-ly\}$. The verb *looked* contains either the past tense morpheme $\{Pas\}$ or the past participle morpheme $\{-en\}$; it is impossible to distinguish one from the other in isolation when the verb is regular. The word *run* could take a number of morphemes (although the particular morphemes that can be added depend on whether the word is used as a noun, as in *The team only got one run today*, or as a verb). The word *impossible* contains an allomorph of the negative prefix morpheme $\{un-\}$. And the word *goodness* contains a nominalization morpheme: $\{-ness\}$.

On the other hand, none of the following words can combine with bound morphemes:

to,　through,　and,　but,　of

They are, consequently, structure words.

We should note here that these examples are not intended to give the reader a means of *discovering* structure words and form words. Discovery procedures are difficult to develop, and they seem to have no practical place in a

pedagogical transformational grammar. The fact, therefore, that most form words can be inflected, and that most
structure words cannot, is not to be taken as part of a definition of these two classes. Rather, such facts are merely
features of the classes. The facts are introduced into this
discussion simply as an aid to the reader in acquiring an
introductory understanding of the difference between form
and structure words.

The case of the auxiliary verb underscores the importance of not using features as a basis for definition or,
which would be even more self-defeating, as a basis for
developing a procedure to discover which words are form
words and which are structure words. Nearly all auxiliary
verbs can be inflected to show the difference between present and past tense (e.g., *may, might; has, had; is, was*), yet
auxiliary verbs are classed with structure words rather
than with form words. This distinction is made by linguists
partly because the primary function of auxiliary verbs is to
indicate a variation in **mood, aspect**, and **voice** *in the main
verb*. Thus, in a sentence such as:

Sentence 3.4   The pterodactyls may be eating the aardvarks.

the auxiliary verbs *may* and *be* indicate, respectively, the
conditional mood and the durative aspect (the so-called
progressive tense). The lexical meaning of the main verb
eat is not changed by their presence.

There is also another way of indicating the difference
between form words and structure words which, in the
author's experience, appeals to students at any grade level.
The distinction is particularly obvious when we attempt to
coin "nonsense words." As Lewis Carroll, to cite only the
most famous example, has demonstrated in "Jabber-
wocky," we can coin nonsense *form* words and the result
will still sound like English:

> 'Twas brillig, and the slithy toves
> Did gyre and gimble in the wabe;
> All mimsy were the borogoves,
> And the mome raths outgrabe.

If this example is too familiar, then consider this one:

> Sentence 3.5   The rinkest lats were oufily spoted to the
> paffest sedams.

All of the form words in this sentence are nonsense words; that is, they have no lexical meaning that we could discover in a dictionary of English. Nonetheless, the sentence can be read to sound like English; that is, it seems to have a basic English structure. To put it still another way, it has *structural* but not *formal* (or *lexical*) meaning.

Suppose, on the other hand, we have a sentence such as the following:

> Sentence 3.6   Cho boys gil sebe toap sitting pe chub wall.

Here some of the words obviously have lexical meaning (that is, we can define *boys, sitting*, and *wall*), but we have no idea of how the words fit together; the structure of the sentence seems to be very different from any English sentence we may have seen or heard before.

One final distinction between form and structure words can be drawn. The class of form words is relatively open; new form words are probably introduced into the language every day, although most of these new words (technically called **neologisms**) do not penetrate the language very deeply and do not last long. Nonetheless, coining form words is easy. For example, if anyone should want a short name for a transformational grammar or for a phrase-structure grammar, he might call the first a "Tragram" and the second a "Phragram." He could then easily add plural morphemes to these words to produce "Tragrams" and "Phragrams." He could also add an **adjectivalization morpheme**, such as {-*ish*}, to produce "Tragramish" and "Phragramish," which might mean something like: "pertaining to transformational grammar" and "pertaining to phrase-structure grammar." And he could easily use these new words in a readily understandable sentence:

> Sentence 3.7   Phragrams contain no tragramish rules.

The class of structure words, however, is relatively closed. Only rarely is a new conjunction, preposition, or auxiliary verb introduced into the language. Moreover, the number of structure words in English is considerably smaller than the number of form words.

3.3   SECOND MODEL GRAMMAR

Our first model grammar can now be expanded to incorporate some of the ideas presented in this chapter. At the same time, we can introduce the notion of transformations. Before giving a transformation, however, we should first discuss the differences between phrase-structure rules and transformational rules.

As Chapter 2 indicates, a phrase-structure rule is an instruction to replace one symbol (e.g., S) by one or more different symbols (e.g., $NP + VP$). In the strictest sense, the S is just a symbol, even though it is sometimes useful to assume that it stands for "sentence." On the other hand, a transformational rule does not merely refer to a symbol, but rather to whatever the symbol stands for. Emmon Bach has a useful analogy that helps make this point clear:

> Consider a copy editor who is told to go through a manuscript and replace all French words with English words. If he interprets this instruction as a [phrase-structure] rule he will go through the manuscript and replace the phrase "all French words" by the phrase "English words." If he interprets it in a way analogous (but not precisely equivalent) to the instruction of a transformation, he will reach for his French-English dictionary.[3]

The first model grammar contained the symbol *Aux* in the phrase-structure rules, but this symbol was not ex-

---

[3] Emmon Bach, *An Introduction to Transformational Grammars* (New York: Holt, Rinehart and Winston, Inc., 1964), p. 61.

panded in any later rules. It can be expanded as follows:

PS 3.5 $Aux \longrightarrow Tn \ (Modal)$

In this rule, Tn stands for the two **tense morphemes** (sometimes called **agreement morphemes**); the parentheses around the symbol $Modal$ indicate that the presence of the modal is optional in the sentence. This rule is still quite limited since it does not indicate that the verbs *to have* and *to be* can also be used as auxiliaries in English; these will be introduced in a later chapter.

The tense morpheme can also be rewritten:

PS 3.9 $Tn \longrightarrow \begin{Bmatrix} Pres \\ Pas \end{Bmatrix}$

This rule indicates that the first verb in the verbal phrase (or the main verb if there is only one verb in the sentence) must be in either the simple present or the simple past tense.

Finally, we can also remove the limitation that all noun phrases must be plural by adding several noun-phrase expansion rules:

PS 3.6 $NP \longrightarrow \begin{Bmatrix} NP_s \\ NP_p \end{Bmatrix}$

PS 3.7 $NP_s \longrightarrow T + N + \emptyset_2$
PS 3.8 $NP_p \longrightarrow T + N + Z_2$

Briefly, rule PS 3.6 says that, when we come to the symbol NP in a derivation, we are to rewrite it as either NP_s (i.e., "noun phrase singular") or NP_p (i.e., "noun phrase plural"). In rule PS 3.7, the symbol NP_s is rewritten as three symbols: $T + N + \emptyset_2$. Here, the T represents the article, e.g., *the*; the N represents the base (uninflected) form of the noun; and the $\emptyset_2$ represents the singular morpheme. Similarly, in rule PS 3.8, the symbol NP_p is rewritten as three symbols:

$T + N + Z_2$. As before, the T and the N represent, respectively, the article and the uninflected form of the noun; the Z_2 represents the plural morpheme.

As a consequence of these changes, we can remove the *NP* class of items from the lexicon and replace it with two other classes:

> *N:* aardvark, pterodactyl, monster, whale
> *T:* the

To derive the full benefit from these new rules, we must add two additional sections to our grammar. This will be as many sections as we will require in this text; later models of the simplified grammar will increase the number of items in any particular section, but will not increase the number of sections. The two final sections we need to add are: (1) transformational rules, and (2) morphographemic rules. The grammar now has the following shape:

> A. Base Rules
>   1. Phrase-Structure Rules
>   2. Lexicon
> B. Transformational Rules
> C. Morphographemic Rules

The base rules generate the deep structure of the sentence. In particular, we apply phrase-structure rules until we have generated a terminal string; then we substitute words from the lexicon for particular symbols in the terminal string. The transformational rules then guarantee that all of the elements in the sentence are in the proper order. And the morphographemic rules (as the Greek roots of this rather awkward word suggest) combine the various morphemes of the derivation into a graphic representation, that is, into the form of written words. If we were interested in how the final sentence was pronounced, rather than in how it is written, we would have a set of **morphophonetic rules** (i.e., rules of pronunciation) rather than **morphographemic rules** (i.e., rules of writing).

The second model grammar contains three transformational rules:

T 3.1 $NP_s + Pres \implies NP_s + Z_1$
T 3.2 $NP_p + Pres \implies NP_p + \emptyset_1$
T 3.3 $Af + v \implies v + Af$
where $Af = Z_1, \emptyset_1,$ or Pas and where $v = Modal, V_i, V_t,$ or V_c

(NOTE: This rule can be applied only *once* in any single derivation.)

These three rules require extended comment. Once the reader understands fully how they operate, however, all further transformational rules will be easily understood also.

We should note first that both the T number and the double arrow ($\implies$) identify the rule as being a **transformation**. More importantly, we should note that, in a transformational rule, there may be more than one symbol to the left of the arrow. Rule T 3.1 says that when a singular noun phrase is followed by the present tense morpheme, then that morpheme is rewritten as Z_1.

Rule T 3.3 is somewhat different. Briefly, it says that whenever we have a particular kind of affix followed by a particular kind of verb, then we are to reverse the order of the affix and the verb so that the affix becomes attached to its proper place at the end of the verb. At this stage of the presentation, we are able to perform this operation no more than once for any single derivation.

In presenting rule T 3.3 to students, the author has found the descriptive term **flip-flop** to be useful. Phrase-structure rules, by their very nature, cannot rearrange (or flip-flop) any elements in a derivational string; transformational rules, on the other hand, can accomplish such a rearrangement. For example, suppose we had been through a derivation and arrived at the following terminal string:

$$T + N + \emptyset_2 + Pas + V_i$$

Rule T 3.1 does not apply to this string because it does not contain the {*Pres*} morpheme. Rule T 3.3 does apply. That is, the string contains an occurrence of *Af* + *v*:

$$\widehat{(Af)} + \widehat{(v)}$$

$$T + N + \emptyset_2 + Pas + V_i$$

Rule T 3.3 says we must rearrange (or flip-flop) the elements *Af* + *v* as follows:

$$\widehat{(v)} + \widehat{(Af)}$$

$$T + N + \emptyset_2 + V_i + Pas$$

This string underlies such sentences as:

The whale danced.
The monster slept.

Further examples of how the transformational rules operate are given later in the chapter after the second model grammar has been presented in detail.

Before presenting the second grammar, however, we must look briefly at the morphographemic rules. These are straightforward, and can best be explained through examples. Suppose, then, that we have applied all the base rules and transformational rules and have produced the following string:

$$the + pterodactyl + Z_2 + devour + Pas + the + monster + \emptyset_2$$

We would then look in the morphographemic rules and discover that *pterodactyl* + Z_2 is to be rewritten as *pterodactyls*; and that *devour* + *Pas* is to be rewritten as *devoured*; and finally that *monster* + $\emptyset_2$ is to be rewritten as *monster*. After performing these operations, we would have produced the sentence:

Sentence 3.8   The pterodactyls devoured the monster.

In short, the morphographemic rules give the shape (i.e., the spelling) of a word after a bound morpheme has been added to the base form of the word.

The following rules, then, are all morphographemic:

$$whale + \emptyset_2 \longrightarrow whale \qquad monster + \emptyset_2 \longrightarrow monster$$
$$whale + Z_2 \longrightarrow whales \qquad monster + Z_2 \longrightarrow monsters$$

$$sleep + Z_1 \longrightarrow sleeps \qquad seem + Z_1 \longrightarrow seems$$
$$sleep + \emptyset_1 \longrightarrow sleep \qquad seem + \emptyset_1 \longrightarrow seem$$
$$sleep + Pas \longrightarrow slept \qquad seem + Pas \longrightarrow seemed$$

$$may + Z_1 \longrightarrow may \qquad see + Z_1 \longrightarrow sees$$
$$may + \emptyset_1 \longrightarrow may \qquad see + \emptyset_1 \longrightarrow see$$
$$may + Pas \longrightarrow might \qquad see + Pas \longrightarrow saw$$

Obviously, most nouns and verbs (and, indeed, most other words) in English are regular. That is, most nouns form their plural by adding -s. Most verbs form the third person singular of the present tense also by adding -s and they generally form the past tense for all persons by adding -ed. We can use this regularity to reduce the size of the morphographemic part of our grammar considerably. That is, we can include specialized rules to take care of all irregular words and then more generalized rules to account for the regular words. And even in the case of the irregular rules, we can frequently generalize a class of words, such as the modals. For example, the following rule will account for all the present tense forms of all modals:

$$Modal + \begin{Bmatrix} Z_1 \\ \emptyset_1 \end{Bmatrix} \longrightarrow Modal$$

As this rule indicates, no modal is inflected in the present tense. For example:

I may	we may
you may	you may
he may	they may

On the other hand, the past tense form of the modals are irregular and must be listed, perhaps as follows:

$$\begin{bmatrix} can \\ may \\ will \end{bmatrix} + Pas \longrightarrow \begin{bmatrix} could \\ might \\ would \end{bmatrix}$$

Notice that, in this rule, we introduce as a new writing symbol, the square bracket: [ ]. Square brackets are always used in pairs; any item on one line in the bracket to the left of the arrow is rewritten as the item on the same line in the bracket to the right of the arrow. Thus, *can + Pas* is to be rewritten as *could*, and *may + Pas* is to be rewritten as *might*, and so on. This convention holds true for all rules within square brackets.

We can now present a complete version of the second simplified model grammar.

A. Base Rules

Phrase Structure

PS 3.1 $S \longrightarrow NP + VP$

PS 3.2 $VP \longrightarrow Aux + MV$

PS 3.3 $MV \longrightarrow V \ (Adv)$

PS 3.4 $V \longrightarrow \begin{Bmatrix} V_i \\ V_t + NP \\ V_c + Adj \end{Bmatrix}$

PS 3.5 $Aux \longrightarrow Tn \ (Modal)$

PS 3.6 $NP \longrightarrow \begin{Bmatrix} NP_s \\ NP_p \end{Bmatrix}$

PS 3.7 $NP_s \longrightarrow T + N + \emptyset_2$

PS 3.8 $NP_p \longrightarrow T + N + Z_2$

PS 3.9 $Tn \longrightarrow \begin{Bmatrix} Pres \\ Pas \end{Bmatrix}$

Lexicon

N: aardvark, pterodactyl, monster, whale, child, man
T: the *Adv:* today *Adj:* lonesome, hungry
V$_i$: sleep, dance, run *V$_t$:* see, devour, frighten
V$_c$: seem, appear *Modal:* may, can, will

B. Transformational Rules

T 3.1 $NP_s + Pres \Longrightarrow NP_s + Z_1$

T 3.2 $NP_p + Pres \Longrightarrow NP_p + \emptyset_1$

T 3.3 $Af + v \implies v + Af$
where $Af = Z_1,\ \emptyset_1,$ or Pas and where $v = Modal,\ V_i,\ V_t,\ V_c$

(NOTE: This rule can be applied only *once* in any single derivation.)

C. Morphographemic Rules

M 3.1 $N + \emptyset_2 \longrightarrow N$
EXAMPLE: $whale + \emptyset_2 \longrightarrow whale$

- -

M 3.2 $N + Z_2 \longrightarrow Ns$
EXAMPLE: $whale + Z_2 \longrightarrow whales$
except: $man + Z_2 \longrightarrow men;\ child + Z_2 \longrightarrow children$

- -

M 3.3 $\begin{bmatrix} Modal \\ \\ V \end{bmatrix} + \emptyset_1 \longrightarrow \begin{bmatrix} Modal \\ \\ V \end{bmatrix}$
EXAMPLE: $seem + \emptyset_1 \longrightarrow seem$

- -

M 3.4 $\begin{bmatrix} Modal \\ \\ V \end{bmatrix} + Z_1 \longrightarrow \begin{bmatrix} Modal \\ \\ Vs \end{bmatrix}$
EXAMPLE: $seem + Z_1 \longrightarrow seems$

- -

M 3.5 $V + Pas \longrightarrow Ved$
EXAMPLE: $seem + Pas \longrightarrow seemed$
except: $\begin{bmatrix} sleep \\ run \\ see \end{bmatrix} + Pas \longrightarrow \begin{bmatrix} slept \\ ran \\ saw \end{bmatrix}$

- -

M 3.6 $\begin{bmatrix} may \\ can \\ will \end{bmatrix} + Pas \longrightarrow \begin{bmatrix} might \\ could \\ would \end{bmatrix}$

Even this highly restricted grammar will generate more than a thousand sentences, all of which are grammatical. The following derivation is typical:

    S

1.	$NP + VP$	(PS 3.1)
2.	$NP + Aux + MV$	(PS 3.2)
3.	$NP + Aux + V$	(PS 3.3)
4.	$NP + Aux + V_t + NP$	(PS 3.4)
5.	$NP + Tn + Modal + V_t + NP$	(PS 3.5)
6.	$NP_s + Tn + Modal + V_t + NP_p$	(PS 3.6)
7.	$T + N + \emptyset_2 + Tn + Modal + V_t + NP_p$	(PS 3.7)
8.	$T + N + \emptyset_2 + Tn + Modal + V_t + T + N + Z_2$	(PS 3.8)
9.	$T + N + \emptyset_2 + Pas + Modal + V_t + T + N + Z_2$	(PS 3.9)

String No. 9 is the terminal string of the phrase-structure derivation. Notice that in line 3 of the derivation we did not choose the optional adverb, but that in line 5 we did choose the optional modal. The grammar will produce grammatical sentences no matter whether the optional elements are or are not chosen.

We now substitute words from the lexicon for the relevant elements in the string:

    10. $the + child + \emptyset_2 + Pas + can + see + the + monster + Z_2$

Neither the first nor the second transformations apply because there is no {*Pres*} morpheme in the string. The third (flip-flop) transformation produces the following string:

    11. $the + child + \emptyset_2 + can + Pas + see + the + monster + Z_2$

Finally, we apply the relevant morphographemic rules:

$child + \emptyset_2 \longrightarrow child$	(M 3.1)
$can + Pas \longrightarrow could$	(M 3.6)

$$monster + Z_2 \longrightarrow monsters \qquad \text{(M 3.2)}$$

These yield the following string:

12. *the + child + could + see + the + monsters*

(In a later model of the grammar we will add a rule that removes the plus signs, capitalizes the first word, and places a period at the end of the string to give Sentence 3.9: *The child could see the monsters.*)

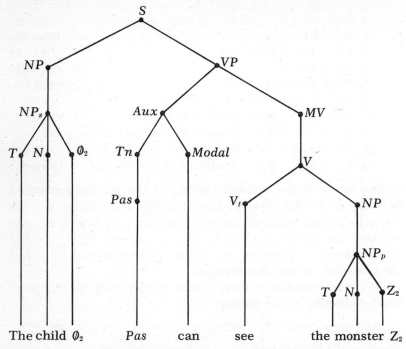

Figure 3.1   Sentence 3.9, deep structure.

We can now amend the earlier statement that each sentence in English can be represented by a single, unique branching tree diagram. Actually, there is a unique tree for every line of the phrase-structure derivation. The most revealing tree is the one which corresponds to the terminal string of the phrase-structure derivation. The second most important tree, for the pedagogical purposes of teachers of English, is the one which represents the sentence after the morphographemic rules have been applied; for all practical purposes this is the "final sentence."

The tree that represents the terminal string of the phrase-structure section of the grammar is a representation of the deep structure; the tree that represents the sentence after the morphographemic rules have been applied shows only the surface structure. For the example given, they have the configurations shown in Figures 3.1 and 3.2.

As indicated in Figure 3.2, Surface Structure, transformations and morphographemic rules tend to obliterate much of the deep structure. Frequently, as we shall see in later chapters, the surface structure fails to indicate fundamental grammatical relationships that are necessary to

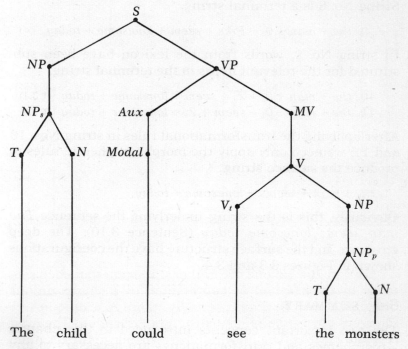

Figure 3.2 Sentence 3.9, surface structure.

an understanding of a sentence. This fact stresses again the importance of transformational analysis, which is the only currently available grammatical analysis that reveals both deep and surface structure fully.

One additional derivation and two more branching trees may make these facts clearer:

$$S$$

1.	$NP + VP$	(PS 3.1)
2.	$NP + Aux + MV$	(PS 3.2)
3.	$NP + Aux + V + Adv$	(PS 3.3)
4.	$NP + Aux + V_c + Adj + Adv$	(PS 3.4)
5.	$NP + Tn + V_c + Adj + Adv$	(PS 3.5)
6.	$NP_s + Tn + V_c + Adj + Adv$	(PS 3.6)
7.	$T + N + \emptyset_2 + Tn + V_c + Adj + Adv$	(PS 3.7)
8.	$T + N + \emptyset_2 + Pres + V_c + Adj + Adv$	(PS 3.9)

String No. 8 is a terminal string.

9. $the + man + \emptyset_2 + Pres + seem + lonesome + today$

In string No. 9, words from the lexicon have been substituted for the relevant items in the terminal string.

10. $the + man + \emptyset_2 + Z_1 + seem + lonesome + today$ (T 3.1)
11. $the + man + \emptyset_2 + seem + Z_1 + lonesome + today$ (T 3.3)

After applying the transformational rules in string Nos. 10 and 11, we need only apply the morphographemic rules to produce the surface string:

$the + man + seems + lonesome + today$

Obviously, this is the string underlying the sentence *The man seems lonesome today* (Sentence 3.10). The deep structure and the surface structure have the configurations shown in Figures 3.3 and 3.4.

3.4 SUMMARY

The two important concepts introduced in this chapter — morphemes and transformations — are necessary to any adequate description of how English operates. To recapitu-

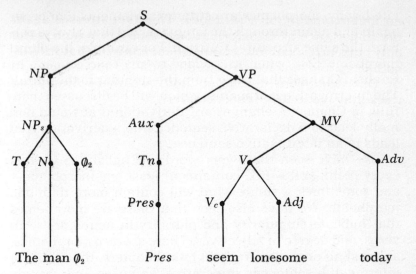

Figure 3.3 Sentence 3.10, deep structure.

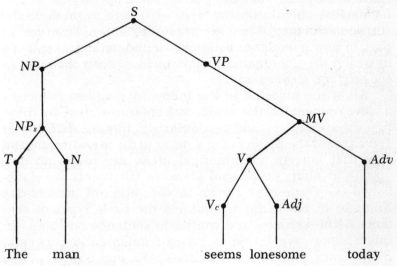

Figure 3.4 Sentence 3.10, surface structure.

late briefly, morphemes are structural elements that occur
again and again through the language and that always perform the same structural function. For example, the plural
morpheme $\{Z_2\}$, when it is added to any **concrete noun** in
English, changes that noun from the singular to the plural.
The interrogative morpheme, which will be discussed more
fully in Chapter 7, changes any derivation that would normally lead to a declarative sentence into a derivation that
leads to an interrogative sentence.

We have seen that every word in English, as well as
every prefix and suffix, contains at least one morpheme—
and sometimes a single word will contain more than one
morpheme. We have also seen that there are morphemes
that indicate singularity and plurality in nouns, tense in
verbs, and degree in adjectives. There are also morphemes,
as we shall note more fully in later chapters, that indicate
interrogative sentences, imperative sentences, and strongly
emphatic sentences. And there are morphemes that indicate present and past participles and negatives. In short,
morphemes are basic in sentence structure.

Transformations, on the other hand, are not structural
elements. Rather, they are grammatical operations. Transformations operate on the deep structure to produce the
surface structure. They are therefore an explanation, in
part, of how a reader or listener can understand a sentence
in which the grammatical relations have been obscured *in
the surface structure.*

All of the material in the following chapters is merely
a development of the basic concepts presented in these
first three chapters, and particularly in this one. In Chapter
1, we traced the history of grammar to the present time and
saw that current grammatical ideas are really an out-
growth of many traditional ideas. In Chapter 2, we established the framework for an investigation of present-day
English; in particular we defined the basic types of sentences (the kernels) and the basic sentence positions. In
this chapter, we introduced two fundamental concepts:
morphemes and transformations. We are now ready to
apply these concepts within the established framework of

the basic sentence types in order to discover more about the structure of English. We are, in short, ready to fulfill our obligation to tradition by adding the insights of today to the accomplishments of the past.

Discussion

1. Compare the inflectional endings of English with either the inflectional endings of Old English or the endings of some foreign language you have studied. Do the same kinds of endings occur (e.g., plural suffixes, past-tense suffixes)? What other kinds of suffixes occur? In comparing the structures of two languages, does it make more sense to compare the morphemes of the languages or the words? Why?

2. Consult one of the standard introductory texts in linguistics for the definition of a "phoneme." How do phonemes compare with morphemes? How do allophones compare with allomorphs? Which are more susceptible to change, phonemes or morphemes? Why? Compare some of the phonemes of Modern English with those of Old English or of a foreign language. Which phonemes do not exist in Modern English? Which phonemes exist in Modern English but do not exist in Old English or in a foreign language?

3. Do other languages have form and structure words similar to those of Modern English? What are some of the morphemes that can be added to English form words? Consult the *Oxford English Dictionary* to determine when the following structure words entered the language: *through, onto, although, must, therefore, should.* Consult the Merriam-Webster's (Second) *International Dictionary* for words marked *obs.* ("obsolete"). Are these obsolete words primarily form words or structure words? Why?

4. Discuss some of the significant differences between transformational rules and phrase-structure rules. If you had a grammar of English and a grammar of some other

Indo-European language, which rules would resemble each other more, the phrase-structure rules, or the transformational rules? Why? On the basis of this evidence, what observations can you make about the differences between deep structure and surface structure?

5. Discuss the thesis that: "discovery procedures . . . seem to have no practical place in a pedagogical transformational grammar." Can you think of situations in which a linguist—or a student—might want to use "discovery procedures" as a means of determining part-of-speech categories for particular words? One philosopher has said that the only kind of definition possible in the twentieth century is "definition by analogy." How does this statement relate to the use of "discovery procedures" by students of English?

Exercises

1. Identify the morphemes (both bound and free) in the following words:

unkindness southwesterly typewriter
inasmuch   illogical   airplanes
contained   jelly   antidisestablishmentarianism

(NOTE: A good etymological dictionary will not only help you to identify morphemes but will also give you some information about their sources.)

2. Which of the following sentences contain the negative morpheme (*Ng*)? the imperative morpheme (*Imp*)? the interrogative morpheme (Q)? the emphatic morpheme (*Emph*)?

1. John will *never* come again.
2. Why won't he?
3. You're not going, are you?
4. Close the *door*!
5. Listen carefully, will you?

3. Identify the phrase-structure rules that are applied in the following derivation:

> S
> 1. $NP + VP$ (PS 3.)
> 2. $NP + Aux + MV$ (PS 3.)
> 3. $NP + Aux + V + Adv$ (PS 3.)
> 4. $NP + Aux + V_t + NP + Adv$ (PS 3.)
> 5. $NP + Tn + V_t + NP + Adv$ (PS 3.)
> 6. $NP_s + Tn + V_t + NP_p + Adv$ (PS 3.)
> 7. $NP_s + Pres + V_t + NP_p + Adv$ (PS 3.)
> 8. $NP_s + Pres + V_t + T + N + Z_2 + Adv$ (PS 3.)
> 9. $T + N + \emptyset_2 + Pres + V_t + T + N + Z_2 + Adv$ (PS 3.)

4. Using the second model grammar, derive the following strings:

> 1. *the + aardvarks + will + sleep + today*
> 2. *the + monsters + may + frighten + the + child*

Draw branching tree diagrams for the deep structure of each of these sentences.

5. Complete the following morphographemic rules:

> *shall* + ⟶ *should*
> *mouse* + Z_2 ⟶
> + Z_2 ⟶ *moose*
> *must* + ⟶ *must*
> + *Pas* ⟶ *hit*
> *have* + Z_1 ⟶

⟨4⟩

Nouns and Nominals

Amo, amas, I love a lass,
As a cedar tall and slender;
Sweet cowslip's grace
Is her nom'native case,
And she's of the feminine gender.

JOHN O'KEEFE, *Amo, Amas*

English is a nominalizing language. There are more operations that transform words and groups of words into noun phrases than there are similar operations for creating new members of any other part-of-speech category. These operations, in fact, permit us to create an indefinite number of noun phrases. This infinite capacity for producing noun phrases suggests that native speakers of English, perhaps intuitively, recognize the primacy of nominals in English.

Robert B. Lees has made an extensive investigation of nouns, substantives, and **nominalizations** (i.e., ways of creating new nominals), and has reported the results of this investigation in a monograph, "The Grammar of English Nominalizations," originally published in 1960 and reprinted twice.[1] Lees gives hundreds of examples of various kinds of nominalizations. Briefly, each of these is a trans-

---

[1] Robert B. Lees, "The Grammar of English Nominalizations," *International Journal of American Linguistics*, Vol. XXVI, No. 3 (July 1960), Part II.

formation that alters or rearranges a word or group of words so that they are able to perform the function of a noun phrase in a sentence. Later in the chapter we shall examine some examples from Lees' report in detail, but we can get an approximate idea of the notion of nominalizations by showing how some of the kernel sentences given in Chapter 2 can be transformed into nominals.

The following sentences were cited earlier as kernels:

Sentence 2.6 The aardvark may be happy.

Sentence 2.8 The forest is sleeping.

Sentence 2.11 The Frenchman drank the wine yesterday.

Suppose we now have a sentence in which the subject is indicated only symbolically:

Sentence 4.1 *Noun Phrase + completely enchanted the poet.*

We can insert a simple noun phrase in the subject position of this sentence:

Sentence 4.1a The girl completely enchanted the poet.

Or we can create substitutes for the noun phrase by transforming the kernel sentences:

Sentence 4.1b The happy aardvark completely enchanted the poet.

Sentence 4.1c The sleeping forest completely enchanted the poet.

Sentence 4.1d The Frenchman drinking the wine completely enchanted the poet.

As these simple examples show, nominalizations are a vital part of language. The ability to create new nominals freely is one of the most powerful and productive talents of a native speaker.

Obviously, there is much here to interest both the linguist and the teacher of English. But we must build up to these and similar transformations gradually.

4.1 RULES FOR NOMINALS

We can most easily begin by referring to phrase-structure rules 3.6, 3.7, and 3.8 of the second model grammar. These rules first expanded the symbol NP into NP_s or NP_p and then expanded these, in turn, into a determiner plus a base noun plus a singular or a plural morpheme. But the noun phrase, defined in this way, is only one of the items that can function as a nominal in a sentence. Consequently, we must enlarge the phrase-structure rules that pertain to noun phrases. In particular, we now want to say:

PS 4.1 $S \longrightarrow Nom + VP$
   (where $Nom =$ "nominal")

PS 4.4 $V \longrightarrow \begin{Bmatrix} V_i \\ V_t + Nom \\ V_c + Adj \end{Bmatrix}$

In addition, we will discard phrase-structure rules PS 3.6 through 3.8, and substitute two new rules in their place.

PS 4.7 $Nom \longrightarrow T + N + N^{\underline{o}}$

PS 4.8 $N^{\underline{o}} \longrightarrow \begin{Bmatrix} \emptyset_2 \\ Z_2 \end{Bmatrix}$

These new rules will obviously change our branching tree diagrams and, in fact, it will make them more accurate. Thus we have the configuration shown in Figure 4.1. Or else, we might replace the $T + N + N^{\underline{o}}$ by an entire nominalization, in which case we would have the configuration shown in the next tree diagram, Figure 4.2. Notice that the entire phrase *the Frenchman drinking the wine* can be traced back to (or is "suspended from") a single node marked *Nom*. We thus have a correct description of the sentence as well as a correct description of the function of the phrase.

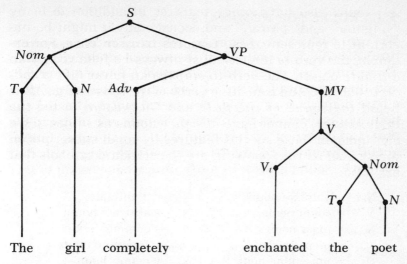

Figure 4.1   Sentence 4.1a, surface structure.

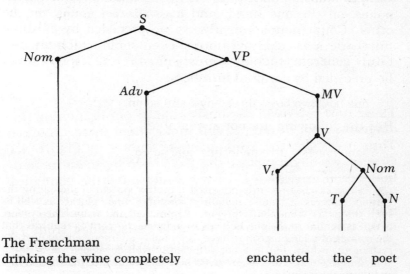

Figure 4.2   Sentence 4.1d, surface structure.

Nouns also have other features in addition to being "singular" and "plural," and occasionally it might be important to represent these features in a sentence. For example, the verb *to amaze* must always be followed by an *animate* object. The verb *to elapse* can never take a *concrete* subject. And transitive verbs of the senses (e.g., *Allen* heard *the sound of the flute* and *Gwendolyn* tasted *the tartar sauce*) cannot have *abstract* nouns as subjects. We can indicate these special features by small subscripts on the symbol N; the following are the standard symbols that are used:[2]

N_{an}	= animate noun	N_{in}	= inanimate
N_c	= count noun	N_{ab}	= abstract noun
N_{mass}	= mass noun	N_{com}	= common noun
N_{pr}	= proper noun	N_{fem}	= feminine noun
N_{masc}	= masculine noun	N_{neu}	= neuter noun

Instead of the usual distinction between concrete nouns and **abstract nouns** found in most school grammars, transformationalists prefer to make a distinction between **count nouns**, on the one hand, and **mass/abstract nouns**, on the other. Count nouns can always be preceded by cardinal numbers; mass/abstract nouns, even some which are certainly concrete (such as *honesty* or *concrete* itself) cannot be preceded by cardinal numbers:

one boy, two boys, three boys, and so on.

But the following are not acceptable:

*one honesty, two honesties, and so on.

_____

[2] Chomsky has recently proposed a matrix system of indicating the various features of nouns, including "singular" and "plural" as well as such things as "common," "proper," "animate," and so on. The system, which is similar to the one he uses to indicate the various features that the sounds of a language may have, is probably an improvement over the system given here, but it is not sufficiently well developed yet to be included in this text. The system given here is adequate to most needs of a pedagogical grammar.

4.2 DETERMINERS

Perhaps because of the importance of nouns, substantives, and nominals in English, the system of **determiners** (i.e., those words which regularly precede nouns) is relatively complex in English. Most school grammars list the articles and other kinds of determiners as a special subclass of adjectives. Transformationalists prefer to restrict adjectives much more narrowly and to introduce a separate category for determiners.

The system of determiners is sufficiently large to have several subclasses. In the discussion which follows, we shall be concerned with the three major subclasses: (1) **regular determiners**, (2) **postdeterminers**, and (3) **predeterminers**. More particularly, we shall be concerned with the way the words in these subclasses fit into patterns.

Regular Determiners. There are three kinds of words in the subclass of regular determiners: **articles, demonstratives**, and **genitives**. Articles and demonstratives can be further subdivided into those which occur with singular and those which occur with plural nouns; the genitives can occur with either singular or plural nouns. The most important of these words are the following:

Articles (*Art*)	Demonstratives (*Dem*)	Genitives (*Gen*)
a (an)	this	my
Ø	that	our
the	these	your
any	those	his
every		her
each		its
some		their
		$Nom + Z_3$

The $Nom + Z_3$ stands for the genitive form (singular or plural) of any nominal. Thus, we can say: *my poem*, or

Phil's poem, or *the boy's poem,* or *that plagiarist's poem.*
Regular determiners occur before nouns:

a boy, an ostrich, the girl, any house, every man
this boy, that ostrich, these girls, those houses
my boy, our ostrich, your girl, his house, her man

The determiners are mutually exclusive. That is, no more
than one regular determiner can precede a noun in a kernel
sentence. There is a corollary to this rule: every noun in
English must be preceded by one regular determiner, although certain nouns are generally preceded by the **zero
article**: $\emptyset$. Thus the following phrases, in which the noun
is preceded by a single determiner, are all grammatical:

a boy, that ostrich, your girl, $\emptyset$ men

On the other hand, the following phrases, in which the
noun is preceded by more than one regular determiner, are
ungrammatical:

*a this boy, *every those ostriches, *this your girl

Such mutual exclusiveness is one fact that distinguishes
the regular determiners, as a class, from the adjectives.
Theoretically, as we shall see, there is no limit to the number of adjectives that can precede a noun.

All of this information concerning determiners can be
incorporated into the phrase-structure part of our grammar. Earlier, we introduced the symbol *Nom*, and rewrote
it as: $T + N + N^{\underline{o}}$. We can make this rule more accurate by
replacing the symbol T by the symbol *Det* (which stands
for regular determiner). Thus, we now have the rule:

PS 4.7 $Nom \longrightarrow Det + N + N^{\underline{o}}$

The rule now says that every noun in English is preceded by a regular determiner of some sort. And we now
need to add a rule to show the permissible kinds of regular
determiners:

PS 4.9 $Det \longrightarrow \begin{Bmatrix} Art \\ Dem \\ Gen \end{Bmatrix}$

In the lexicon, we will list the real English words that can replace these symbols in a derivation; these words, of course, will include those given in the lists of articles, demonstratives, and genitives that we have just examined.

Suppose, then, that we had a sentence with the following line in its derivation:

1. $Det + N + N^o + Pas + V_t + Det + N + N^o$

This string might lead to a sentence such as *The man saw the girl*. However, we can now replace the symbol *Det* by an article other than *the*, or by a demonstrative or a genitive. That is, in the next line of the derivation we might have:

2. $Dem + N + N^o + Pas + V_t + Gen + N + N^o$

and this string would lead to a sentence such as *That man saw your girl*.

Before leaving the discussion of regular determiners we should note that there is a very small class of words, called **prearticles**, which as their name suggests can precede articles (or demonstratives or genitives) including the zero article. The most important of these prearticles are: all, only, both, just.

    all the boys, only that boy, both those girls
    just my speed, all ∅ boys

The zero article, of course, appears only in the deep structure of a sentence and not in the final—or surface—structure.

We can incorporate the optional prearticle into the phrase-structure rule which rewrites *Det* by enclosing it within parentheses on the right side of the arrow.

PS 4.9a $Det \longrightarrow (Preart) \begin{Bmatrix} Art \\ Dem \\ Gen \end{Bmatrix}$

Postdeterminers.   A close examination of English reveals that there is another class of words which follows the regular determiners in an underlying string and which precedes the adjectives. These words, called **postdeter-**

miners, not only follow regular determiners but they also have another unique characteristic: they can co-occur with themselves but only in a fixed order. That is, postdeterminers are different from regular determiners because there can be only one regular determiner before any noun in a matrix sentence while there can be two postdeterminers in addition to the regular determiner. Postdeterminers differ from regular adjectives because adjectives can occur in almost any order while the order of the postdeterminers is fixed.

Like the regular determiners, there are three kinds of postdeterminers:

Ordinals (*Ord*)	Cardinals (*Card*)	Superlatives and Comparatives (*Comp*)
first	one	more
second	two	most
third	three	fewer
fourth	four	fewest
(etc.)	(etc.)	less
next	several	least
last	many	least
final	few	

The postdeterminers can co-occur with determiners:

the first orange, those three statues, some more gravy

They can also co-occur with each other, but only in the order indicated:

the first two azaleas, the last several months

There are some restrictions on the occurrence of postdeterminers that need not concern us in this introductory presentation. We may note in passing, however, that ordinals and cardinals do not both occur with comparatives, and that superlatives are rarely—if ever—preceded by either ordinals or cardinals. And there are also some apparent exceptions to the rule of invariable order:

the two second basemen, the four final examinations

In these examples, however, the phrases *second basemen* and *final examinations* are actually nominals, as we can see in the following examples (where the hyphens are added for clarity):

the second two second-basemen
the final four final-examinations

Thus, we can now rewrite phrase-structure rule PS 4.9a to include postdeterminers. Note that sometimes the post-determiners are preceded by the zero article ($\emptyset$, as in *one mule* or *many hands*):

$$\text{PS 4.9b} \quad Det \longrightarrow (Preart) \begin{Bmatrix} Art \\ Dem \\ Gen \end{Bmatrix} (Postdet)$$

We can also add a rule listing the postdeterminers in the proper order:

$$\text{PS 4.11} \quad Postdet \longrightarrow (Ord)\,(Card)\,(Comp)$$

The parentheses around *Postdet* in PS 4.9b indicate that the presence of postdeterminers before a noun is optional. The parentheses in PS 4.11 indicate that any given post-determiner is also optional. Of course, if we choose the symbol *Postdet* when we come to rule PS 4.9b in a deriva-tion, then we must also choose one or more of the symbols in rule PS 4.11. And if we choose more than one symbol in rewriting rule PS 4.11, then we must observe the occur-rence restrictions and also maintain the fixed order indi-cated in the rule.

To return to the derivation which we used as an ex-ample in discussing the regular determiners, let us sup-pose we had the string:

1. $Det + N + N^{\underline{o}} + Pas + V_t + Det + N + N^{\underline{o}}$

We have already seen that, if we select only regular determiners to replace the symbol *Det*, we could produce a sentence such as *That man saw your girl.* Suppose, however, we also select the optional item *Postdet.* Later in the derivation, we might have a string such as:

2. $Dem + Card + N + N^{\underline{o}} + Pas + V_t + Gen + Ord + Card + N + N^{\underline{o}}$

And this string would lead to a sentence such as *That last man saw your first two girls.*

Predeterminers. But our analysis of the determiner system of English is still not complete. In addition to the regular determiners and the postdeterminers, there is another class of items in the determiner system: the **predeterminers.** As their descriptive name suggests, they precede both the regular determiners and the postdeterminers.

Like the other two classes of determiners, the predeterminers have a unique feature: they are invariably separated from the regular determiners by the word *of.* Since no other word is ever used to separate predeterminers from regular determiners, we can consider *of* — in this case — to be a special morpheme: the **predeterminer morpheme.**

As a class, the predeterminers include most of the regular determiners and postdeterminers as well as certain **nouns of quantity.** That is, if we have a regular determiner such as *some* or *any* or a postdeterminer such as *one* or *most*, and if such words are separated from a following determiner by *of*, then they are said to be predeterminers. This is most easily seen through illustration. In the following examples, the predeterminers and the predeterminer morpheme are given in italics:

all of the emperors
some of those owls
most of my freckles
each of my ships
the first of those three bubbles
just the last two of my first five children

And in addition to the regular determiners and postdeterminers, there are certain nouns of quantity that function with *of* as predeterminers:

> *a quart of* molasses
> *a mile of* spaghetti
> *only the first two barrels of* oil

Nouns of quantity, when used as predeterminers, almost always cause problems in teaching English. We have already noted that the subject and verb must agree in number and have included an agreement morpheme in the grammar to guarantee the needed agreement. Suppose we have the following sentence:

Sentence 4.2   The milk was shipped to the city in a railroad car.

The subject, *milk*, is a mass noun and mass nouns take singular verbs in English. But suppose we had this sentence:

Sentence 4.3   The two quarts of milk were delivered by bobsled.

Here the verb is plural to agree with *quarts*. Yet we are still talking about *milk*; in fact, we are talking about a much smaller quantity of milk than in Sentence 4.2, which has a singular verb. Consequently, it is sometimes useful to make a distinction between the logical subject of a sentence (*milk* in both these cases) and the grammatical subject. Generally, the logical and grammatical subjects will be the same. When we have a predeterminer, however, they may be different. The verb generally agrees with the grammatical subject.[3]

---

[3] This rule is probably undergoing a change. For example, most native speakers say *A number of boys were going,* where the verb agrees with the logical subject when the predeterminer incorporates an indefinite article. On the other hand, most speakers use a singular verb when the predeterminer incorporates a definite article: *The number of boys was small.*

This interesting distinction points up one important fact about language. As some unknown critic has said, "History is not logical; it is merely chronological." Language *is* logical, but the logic of language may be, and frequently is, very different from the logic of the real world. And this is another reason why we use some of the methods of modern symbolic logic to indicate some of the rules of grammar.[4] The various kinds of determiners can be incorporated into the determiner phrase-structure rule:

$$\text{PS 4.9c} \quad Det \longrightarrow (Predet)\,(Preart) \begin{Bmatrix} Art \\ Dem \\ Gen \end{Bmatrix} (Postdet)$$

We now need to add a rule to account for the various kinds of predeterminers:

$$\text{PS 4.12} \quad Predet \longrightarrow \begin{Bmatrix} (Preart) \begin{Bmatrix} Art \\ Dem \\ Gen \end{Bmatrix} (Postdet) \\ N_{quan} \end{Bmatrix} + of$$

The symbol N_{quan}, standing for "noun of quantity," covers words such as *mile, barrel, quart, slice, wedge, piece, gallon, peck,* and so on.

Obviously, there are many restrictions on the occurrence of determiners (including predeterminers and postdeterminers) in real English sentences. For example, the article *a* must always be used with a singular noun; *both* can be used only with a plural noun (or with two singular nouns conjoined by *and*); singular nouns of quantity must be preceded by one or more determiners, and so forth. This text, however, does not pretend to be more than an introduction to a grammar of English. Consequently, we have room for no more than a few of these restrictions. Native speakers of English, interestingly enough, seldom have

---

[4] There are some Slavic languages, for example, that have three numbers (singular, dual, and plural) instead of two as in English (singular and plural). Singular nouns take singular verbs; dual nouns take plural verbs; and plural nouns, strangely enough, take singular verbs.

any difficulty with the system of determiners. Some speakers for whom English is a second language have considerable difficulty with the English determiner system, particularly if their own language lacks articles. The number of such rules required in a pedagogical grammar depends largely upon the purpose of the grammar. For native speakers of English, the number is probably small; for nonnative speakers, it may be quite large indeed. For the purposes of the third model grammar we shall omit many of the refinements of the system.

4.2a NOUNS

We are now ready to turn to a more detailed investigation of nouns, but first we need to introduce the notion of PRO forms. The usefulness of this notion will become clearer as we develop it throughout the remainder of the text. At this point we need only to say that *Nom* can be rewritten as:

$$4.7a \quad Nom \longrightarrow \begin{Bmatrix} PRO_D + PRO_N \\ Det + N + N^{\underline{o}} \end{Bmatrix}$$

where PRO_D stands for the PRO form of determiners (e.g., *SOME*) and PRO_N stands for the PRO form of nouns (e.g., *ONE, BODY, THING*). In the lexicon, the PRO form of the determiner is replaced by *SOME*, and the PRO_N is replaced by either *ONE* or *BODY* (for animate) or *THING* (for inanimate). Thus, the rules will generate:

SOME + ONE   (and)   *SOME + THING*

And the morphographemic rules will combine these to form:

SOMEONE   (and)   *SOMETHING*

With PRO forms available to us, we can now make the important statement that *no transformation ever deletes an irrecoverable item.* In other words, PRO forms permit us

to construct branching tree diagrams for terminal strings
of kernel sentences that have been simplified by various
transformations.

We may illustrate this by taking two sentences that
have been simplified by transformations.

Sentence 4.4   For want of a nail, the battle was lost.
Sentence 4.5   What was whispered behind the bushes?

Underlying each of these examples is a kernel sentence
containing a PRO form:

Sentence 4.4a   *SOMEONE* lost the battle for want of a nail.
Sentence 4.5a   *SOMEONE* whispered *SOMETHING* behind
the bushes.

We can easily draw branching tree diagrams for both of
these kernel sentences. The prepositional phrases, of
course, would trace back to (or be "suspended from") the
optional *Adv* at the end of the verb phrase.[5]

PRO forms are also obviously related to pronouns in
English. In a pedagogical grammar, we can treat pronouns
as a particular subclass of PRO forms. Like PRO forms,
they are never preceded by determiners (since, in one
sense, the determiner *SOME* is built into the PRO form from
which the pronoun is derived). And they illustrate particularly well a second feature of the PRO form rule:

1. No transformation ever deletes an irrecoverable item.
2. Repeated items (which are easily recoverable) are either
   deleted completely or else are replaced by the pronoun
   form of PRO forms.

The first part of the rule has already been illustrated. The
second part has two subparts, each of which can be easily

---

[5] As the second example indicates, PRO forms will be useful when we
come to discuss questions. Thus, *SOMEONE* and *SOMETHING* are related to *who* and *what*. We will also investigate other PRO forms, such as
SOMEPLACE and *SOMETIME*, which are related to *where* and *when*.

illustrated. The first subpart indicates why all the following
sentences are grammatical in English:

Sentence 4.6a   Sarah has eaten more snails than Michael
has eaten.

Sentence 4.6b   Sarah has eaten more snails than Michael
has.

Sentence 4.6c   Sarah has eaten more snails than Michael.

In Sentence 4.6b we have deleted the verb *eaten*, and in
Sentence 4.6c the verbal phrase *has eaten*. These deletions
are permissible in English because the items deleted are
easily recoverable. This is what we generally mean when
we say that "something is understood" in a sentence. And
it is more than a coincidence that we use the word *something* — a variant of the PRO form *SOMETHING* — in such
an explanation.

The second subpart of the rule accounts for the fact
that there are no sentences such as **John saw John in the
mirror*, where both occurrences of *John* refer to the same
man. As we shall see, there is an obligatory transformation
which changes this sentence into *John saw himself in the
mirror*.

The second subpart of the rule also accounts for the
fact that the following sentence is grossly ungrammatical:

Sentence 4.7a   *When Bob and Pat come home, Bob puts
Bob's car in Bob's and Pat's garage and Pat puts Pat's
car in front of Bob's and Pat's house.

In short, the second PRO form rule says that repeated items
such as those in the ungrammatical sentence must be replaced by pronouns:

Sentence 4.7b   When Bob and Pat come home, he puts his
car in their garage and she puts her car in front of their
house.

This long discussion has accounted for the occurrence

of nouns, PRO forms, and pronouns in English. The combination of $Det + N + N^{\underline{o}}$ can be very short:

Sentence 4.8a   Children must attend school.

In this case, both nouns are preceded by the zero determiner. However, the combination can be rather long:

Sentence 4.8b   Just the last two of my first five children must attend school.

Here all of the words preceding *children* are part of the determiner system. We can also replace the entire nominal with a pronoun:

Sentence 4.8c   They must attend school.

And as a kernel sentence underlying the question *Who must attend school?* we have the PRO form:

Sentence 4.8d   *SOMEONE* must attend school.

4.3   ADJECTIVES

So far we have said nothing about **adjectives** that occur with nouns. To do so, we must first open the door to the most powerful rule in English, the rule which gives the language its infinite variety.

Very briefly, the rule says that the symbol *Nom* dominates an optional sentence. Symbolically, the rule can be stated as follows:

$$\text{PS 4.7a} \quad Nom \longrightarrow \begin{Bmatrix} PRO_D + PRO_N \\ Det + N + N^{\underline{o}} \end{Bmatrix} (+S)$$

Under certain conditions, this rule permits us to **embed** one sentence into another. This embedding process is, in a transformational generative grammar, the source of all adjective modifiers and subordinate clauses in English. We may illustrate this most easily with an example taken from Chomsky. Suppose we have the kernel sentence:

Sentence 4.9a   God created the world.

In some derivational string, this sentence could also have the form:

Sentence 4.9b   God (+S) created the world (+S)

Now suppose that we substitute two new sentences for the S symbols in the string, giving:

Sentence 4.9c   1. God (God is invisible) created the world (the world is visible).

An obligatory transformation would take a string of this sort, delete the easily recoverable (i.e., repeated) items, and give:[6]

Sentence 4.9d   Invisible God created the visible world.

Every adjective that occurs in a prenominal position is introduced into that position from an embedded sentence that has the form of the first kernel given in Chapter 2: *Nom + be + Pred*, where the symbol *Pred* stands, in this case, for *Adj*. Thus, underlying Sentence 4.9d is the string:

God (*God + is + Adj*) created the world (*the world + is + Adj*)

At this point, it is useful to introduce two new terms: **matrix** and **constituent**. Traditional grammarians use the terms independent and dependent clauses; the two new terms are somewhat more descriptive and precise. The basic sentence, traditionally called an independent clause, is called a matrix sentence by most transformationalists. The sentence which is embedded, traditionally called the dependent clause, is called a constituent sentence by transformationalists. In English, a constituent sentence of some sort can be embedded after any noun in a matrix sentence. This fact, as we shall see, has far-reaching implications.

---

[6] In French, from which Chomsky originally drew this example, the adjective remains behind the noun: *Le Dieu invisible a creé le monde visible*. The deep structures of the French and English sentences are identical; the transformations in the two languages simply order the adjectives differently.

We can now write a transformation for embedding adjectives into any matrix sentence. Anywhere that we have an occurrence of $Det + N + N^{\underline{o}}$ (+S) where the embedded S has the form $Det + N + N^{\underline{o}} + be + Adj$, and where the noun of the matrix is identical to the noun of the constituent, we can rewrite the original string as $Det + Adj + N + N^{\underline{o}}$. Symbolically, the transformation is written as follows:

T 4.4 $Det + N_{matrix} + N^{\underline{o}} (+ Det + N_{const} + N^{\underline{o}} + be + Adj)$
   $\Longrightarrow Det + Adj + N_{matrix} + N^{\underline{o}}$
   where $N_{matrix} + N^{\underline{o}} = N_{const} + N^{\underline{o}}$

There are no constraints, except those of style, on the number of times this transformation may be applied to a particular sentence.

One further illustration might be useful. Suppose we have a derivation with the following string:

1. $Det + N + N^{\underline{o}} (+S) + Pas + V_t + Det + N + N^{\underline{o}}$

This might lead to the following string:

2. $the + man (+S) + saw + the + girl$

Suppose now we replace the optional S with a constituent sentence that has the same subject as the matrix sentence:

3. $the + man (+ the + man + is + tall) + saw + the + girl$

This string satisfies the conditions of T 4.4 and we can therefore move the adjective in the constituent to a prenominal position in the matrix and then delete the repeated items in the constituent to give:

4. $the + tall + man + saw + the + girl$

The process of incorporating an optional S after every *Nom* in the grammar adds a property known as **recursiveness** to the grammar. The recursiveness makes the grammar capable of producing an infinite number of sentences. The term simply means that we go through all the rules of the grammar once. If we elect the optional S, then we go through all the rules again, and if that time we elect another optional S, then we go through all the rules a third time, and so forth. In short, a recursive rule is one which enables us to trace our way through the grammar again and again.

4.4   SUBORDINATE CLAUSES

The process of subordinating sentences is also related to the recursive S which occurs optionally after every English nominal. Before presenting the transformation, however, we must first turn back to rule PS 4.9c which generates determiners. We want to enlarge the rule once more to include an optional *wh-* which generates the forms traditionally known as relative pronouns. Thus, the rule should read:

$$\text{PS 4.9d}\quad Det \longrightarrow \left\{ \begin{array}{l} wh\text{-} \\ (Predet)\,(Preart) \left\{ \begin{array}{l} Art \\ Dem \\ Gen \end{array} \right\} (Postdet) \end{array} \right\}$$

If we select *wh-* in this rule, we cannot choose any other symbol.[7]

Suppose we have a matrix sentence such as the following:

Sentence 4.10   *The + man (+S) + came + from + Calcutta*

We may use the optional S to embed a subordinate clause into the matrix. We might, then, enlarge Sentence 4.10 as follows:

Sentence 4.10a   *The + man (+ Det + man + likes + balloons) + came + from + Calcutta*

If the noun in the matrix is identical to the noun in the con-

---

[7] Actually, the determiner system is slightly more complex than this rule indicates, since pronouns can be preceded by some kinds of predeterminers. *Darwin gave a party for* all of *them. He built three houses, the first two of* which are already sold.

stituent, we may embed the constituent as a subordinate clause by selecting *wh-* as the determiner:

Sentence 4.10b   *The + man (+ wh- + man + likes + balloons)*
+ came + from + Calcutta

Since the identical nouns are animate and since the noun in the constituent is the subject of its sentence, we combine *wh- + man* to give *who*:

Sentence 4.10c   *The + man + who + likes + balloons + came*
+ from + Calcutta

This sentence, of course, can also be shown in a branching tree diagram:

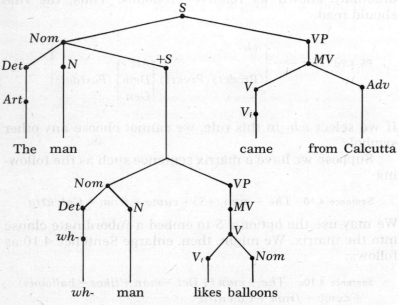

Figure 4.3   Sentence 4.10b.

Notice that, similar to the case of embedding adjectives, we can only embed a subordinate clause if the nouns in the matrix and constituent sentences are identical.

We can now give the subordinate clause transformation more formally:

$$\text{T 4.5} \quad wh\text{-} + \begin{bmatrix} N_{an} \\ N_{in} \end{bmatrix} \Longrightarrow \begin{bmatrix} who \\ which,\ that \end{bmatrix}$$

In its present form, transformation T 4.5 can only be used when the noun in the constituent is also the subject of the constituent. We shall remove this restriction later.

4.5 APPOSITIVES AND LOCATIVES

In addition to adjectives, there are two other kinds of words that can follow the verb *to be* in the kernel sentence illustrated in Chapter 2. Specifically, the verb *to be* can be followed by nominals, adjectives, and adverbs of location. To cite the earlier examples again, we can say:

Sentence 2.5   The animal is an aardvark.
Sentence 2.6   The aardvark may be happy.
Sentence 2.7   The aardvark has been there.

Thus, as already suggested in Chapter 2, we shall have a phrase-structure rule which says:

$$\text{PS 4.6} \quad Pred \longrightarrow \begin{Bmatrix} Nom \\ Adj \\ Loc \end{Bmatrix}$$

Predicate adjectives, as we have already seen, can be introduced from a constituent sentence into a position immediately preceding a noun in a matrix sentence. We can also introduce predicate nominals and predicate adverbs of location from a constituent sentence into a noun-modifying position of a matrix sentence; nominals and adverbs, however, *follow* the nouns they modify. Nominals introduced in this fashion are traditionally called **nouns in apposition**.

Again, we can most easily present the operation through

illustration. Suppose we have two sentences, a matrix and constituent:

Sentence 4.11a   My mother-in-law likes roses. (matrix)
Sentence 4.11b   My mother-in-law is a telephone operator. (constituent)

The constituent sentence contains a predicate nominal. The subjects of the two sentences are identical. Consequently, we may embed the predicate nominal of the constituent sentence after the subject of the matrix sentence; the resulting construction is known as a noun in apposition:

Sentence 4.11c   My mother-in-law, a telephone operator, likes roses.

We may do the same with predicate adverbs of location. In the example given below, the adverb is actually an adverbial prepositional phrase as are most adverbs of location in a transformational grammar of English:

Sentence 4.12a   The frost is lovely.
Sentence 4.12b   The frost is on the pumpkin.

These combine to produce:

Sentence 4.12c   The frost on the pumpkin is lovely.

The transformations for these two operations are relatively simple:

T 4.7 $Det + N_{matrix} + N^{\underline{o}} \ (+ Det + N_{const} + N^{\underline{o}} + be + Nom)$
    $\Longrightarrow Det + N_{matrix} + N^{\underline{o}} + , + Nom + ,$
    where $N_{matrix} + N^{\underline{o}} = N_{const} + N^{\underline{o}}$

T 4.6 $Nom_{matrix} \ (+ Nom_{const} + be + Loc) \Longrightarrow Nom_{matrix} + Loc$
    where $Nom_{matrix} = Nom_{const}$

Before completing this long discussion of the noun phrase in English, we should look briefly at two forms related to the appositive: the **reflexive** and **intensive pronouns**. As we have already suggested, the reflexive pronoun is related to the PRO form rule; the intensifying pronouns are also a special case of the PRO form rule.

Briefly, the rule said that repeated items must either be deleted or replaced by a pronoun. This is precisely what happens in the case of these special pronouns.

The name intensifying pronoun is a good one; it indicates that the constituent sentence is identical to the entire matrix sentence. Thus we have:

> Sentence 4.13a   Rupert (Rupert drank the coffee) drank the coffee.

In this case, the entire constituent sentence is replaced by the intensifier *himself*.

> Sentence 4.13b   Rupert himself drank the coffee.

And since the intensifier pronoun serves to intensify the meaning of the entire sentence, it moves about more freely than regular appositives:

> Sentence 4.13c   Rupert drank the coffee himself.

In the case of intensifiers, the bound morpheme {-*self*} actually represents everything else in the sentence exclusive of the nominal (which is represented by the pronoun).

Reflexives are less movable. In this case, the bound morpheme {-*self*} indicates only that the nominal for which the pronoun is substituting is identical to the nominal which is the subject of the sentence.

4.6   THIRD MODEL GRAMMAR

The material presented in this chapter is too extensive to be conveniently included in a model grammar. In particular, we would have to write a great many conditions on the occurrence of various items such as determiners. Consequently, the model grammar that follows is considerably simplified. It is intended primarily to illustrate the operation of embedding. For this reason, it omits the rules we have developed for PRO forms and for predeterminers and postdeterminers. Furthermore, it assumes that the person

using the rules is familiar with the restrictions on articles
before singular and plural nouns. In short, the third model
grammar has a pedagogical purpose only; it is not a scientific grammar.

In addition to the new transformations presented earlier in this chapter, we also need to include a means of
generating kernel sentences containing the verb *to be* as a
main verb. As we noticed in the discussion of the four
forms of kernel sentences in Chapter 1, and in the presentation of the first model grammar in Chapter 2, the verb *to
be* has unique properties that would have needlessly complicated the initial presentation of a model grammar. Now,
however, we need to incorporate these unique properties
into the grammar so we can obtain the necessary recursiveness that is an identifying feature of a transformational
generative grammar. Consequently, we will rewrite rule
PS 3.3 of the second model grammar as follows:

$$\text{PS 4.3} \quad MV \longrightarrow \begin{Bmatrix} be + Pred \\ V \end{Bmatrix} (Loc) (Tm)$$

where *Pred* stands for those predicates which can follow the
verb *to be*; *Loc* stands for adverbs of location (or place);
and *Tm* stands for adverbs of time.

We also need a rule for rewriting *Pred*, and this should
appear before the rule which rewrites *Nom*:

$$\text{PS 4.6} \quad Pred \longrightarrow \begin{Bmatrix} Nom \\ Adj \\ Loc \end{Bmatrix}$$

As this rule indicates, the predicate that follows the verb
to be used as a main verb can be a nominal (*He is my
brother*), an adjective (*She is delirious*), or an adverb of
location (*It is here*).

The rules that follow will still not generate more than
a small part of the English verb system; this will be the
subject of the following chapter. Not all the restrictions
are rigorously listed, particularly when native speakers of

English seldom, if ever, violate the restrictions. In contrast, however, to the first two versions of the model grammar, this version will generate an infinite number of sentences, and if all the restrictions – both stated and assumed – are observed, all the sentences will be grammatical.

A. Base Rules

Phrase Structure

PS 4.1 $S \longrightarrow Nom + VP$

PS 4.2 $VP \longrightarrow Aux + MV$

PS 4.3 $MV \longrightarrow \begin{Bmatrix} be + Pred \\ V \end{Bmatrix} (Loc) (Tm)$

PS 4.4 $V \longrightarrow \begin{Bmatrix} V_i \\ V_t + Nom \\ V_c + Adj \end{Bmatrix}$

PS 4.5 $Aux \longrightarrow Tn(Modal)$

PS 4.6 $Pred \longrightarrow \begin{Bmatrix} Nom \\ Adj \\ Loc \end{Bmatrix}$

PS 4.7 $Nom \longrightarrow Det + N + N^{\underline{o}} (+S)$

PS 4.8 $N^{\underline{o}} \longrightarrow \begin{Bmatrix} \emptyset_2 \\ Z_2 \end{Bmatrix}$

PS 4.9 $Det \longrightarrow \begin{Bmatrix} wh- \\ Art \\ Dem \end{Bmatrix}$

PS 4.10 $Tn \longrightarrow \begin{Bmatrix} Pres \\ Pas \end{Bmatrix}$

Lexicon

N: aardvark, pterodactyl, monster, whale, child, man, creature, witch, dragon

Art: a (an), the, any, every, each, some

Dem: this, that, these, those

V_i: sleep, dance, run, come

V_t: see, devour, frighten, entertain

V_c: seem, appear, become

$Modal$: may, can, will

Adj: lonesome, hungry, happy, angry

Loc: here, there, in the forest

Tm: today, at midnight

B.   Transformational Rules

T 4.1 $\begin{bmatrix} NP_s \\ \\ NP_p \end{bmatrix} + Pres \implies \begin{bmatrix} NP_s + Z_1 \\ \\ NP_p + \emptyset_1 \end{bmatrix}$

T 4.2 $Af + v \implies v + Af$
where $Af = Z_1, \emptyset_1,$ or Pas
   $v = be, V_i, V_t,$ or V_c
NOTE: T 4.2 applies only once for each S.

T 4.3 $\begin{bmatrix} NP_s \\ \\ NP_p \end{bmatrix} + be + Pas \implies \begin{bmatrix} NP_s + was \\ \\ NP_p + were \end{bmatrix}$

T 4.4 $Det + N_{matrix} + N^{\underline{o}} (+ Det + N_{const} + N^{\underline{o}} + be + Adj) \implies Det + Adj + N_{matrix} + N^{\underline{o}}$
where $N_{matrix} + N^{\underline{o}} = N_{const} + N^{\underline{o}}$

T 4.5 $wh\text{-} + \begin{bmatrix} N_{an} \\ \\ N_{in} \end{bmatrix} \implies \begin{bmatrix} who \\ \\ which, that \end{bmatrix}$

T 4.6 $Nom_{matrix} (+ Nom_{const} + be + Loc) \implies Nom_{matrix} + Loc$
where $Nom_{matrix} = Nom_{const}$

T 4.7 $Det + N_{matrix} + N\underline{o} \; (+ Det + N_{const} + N\underline{o} + be + Nom)$
$\Longrightarrow Det + N_{matrix} + N\underline{o} + , + Nom + ,$
where $N_{matrix} + N\underline{o} = N_{const} + N\underline{o}$

C. Morphographemic Rules

By this time, the reader should be sufficiently familiar with the morphographemic rules so that we can omit them from the model grammar.

Derivations. Because of the complexity of this third model grammar, it will probably help if we have some notion of where the derivations are leading. As examples, then, we shall derive the following three sentences:

Sentence 4.14   The creature, a dragon, was angry today.

Sentence 4.15   Those witches who dance at midnight will become hungry.

Sentence 4.16   The pterodactyls in the forest entertained some lonesome children.

The first example, Sentence 4.14, has a noun in apposition to the subject. The second example, Sentence 4.15, has an embedded relative clause after the subject. And the third example, Sentence 4.16, has an embedded *Loc* after the first noun and an embedded *Adj* before the second noun. Consequently, the first and second examples each require one constituent sentence to be embedded into the matrix; the third example requires two constituent sentences.

Derivation of Sentence 4.14

Matrix Sentence
    S

1. $Nom + VP$		(PS 4.1)
2. $Nom + Aux + MV$		(PS 4.2)
3. $Nom + Aux + be + Pred + Tm$		(PS 4.3)
4. $Nom + Tn + be + Pred + Tm$		(PS 4.5)
5. $Nom + Tn + be + Adj + Tm$		(PS 4.6)

6. $Det + N + N^{\underline{u}}\,(+S) + Tn + be + Adj + Tm$ (PS 4.7)
7. $Det + N + \emptyset_2\,(+S) + Tn + be + Adj + Tm$ (PS 4.8)
8. $Art + N + \emptyset_2\,(+S) + Tn + be + Adj + Tm$ (PS 4.9)
9. $Art + N + \emptyset_2\,(+S) + Pas + be + Adj + Tm$ (PS 4.10)

Line No. 9 is the terminal string of the phrase-structure derivation of the kernel (matrix) sentence. By substituting words from the lexicon we get:

10. $the + creature + \emptyset_2\,(+S) + Pas + be + angry + today$

Transformation T 4.2 will rearrange $Pas + be$ to give $be + Pas$, and the transformation T 4.3 will rewrite $be + Pas$ to give was:

11. $the + creature + \emptyset_2\,(+S) + was + angry + today$

There is one morphographemic rule which applies:

$creature + \emptyset_2 \longrightarrow creature$

This rule gives:

12. $the + creature\,(+S) + was + angry + today$

Line No. 12 gives the surface structure of the matrix sentence. We must now embed a sentence that has the shape: *The creature is a dragon.* The terminal string of this constituent sentence has the shape:

1a. $Art + N + \emptyset_2 + Pres + be + Art + N + \emptyset_2$

After substituting words from the lexicon and applying the appropriate morphographemic rules and transformations, we get:

2a. $the + creature + is + a + dragon$

We now embed this constituent sentence into the matrix sentence:

13. $the + creature\,(+ the + creature + is + a + dragon)$
$+ was + angry + today$

This string satisfies the requirements of transformation T 4.7, so we may apply it to get the final string:

14. *the + creature + , + a + dragon + , + was + angry + today*

By removing the plus signs and applying the appropriate rules of punctuation we get:

15. The creature, a dragon, was angry today.

Derivation of Sentence 4.15.

Matrix Sentence

S

1. $Nom + VP$		(PS 4.1)
2. $Nom + Aux + MV$		(PS 4.2)
3. $Nom + Aux + V$		(PS 4.3)
4. $Nom + Aux + V_c + Adj$		(PS 4.4)
5. $Nom + Tn + Modal + V_c + Adj$		(PS 4.5)
6. $Det + N + N^{\underline{o}} (+S) + Tn + Modal + V_c + Adj$		(PS 4.7)
7. $Det + N + Z_2 (+S) + Tn + Modal + V_c + Adj$		(PS 4.8)
8. $Dem + N + Z_2 (+S) + Tn + Modal + V_c + Adj$		(PS 4.9)
9. $Dem + N + Z_2 (+S) + Pres + Modal + V_c + Adj$		(PS 4.10)

Line No. 9 is the terminal string of the phrase-structure derivation of the matrix sentence. By substituting words from the lexicon and applying the appropriate transformations and morphographemic rules we get:

10. *those + witches (+S) + will + become + hungry*

Line No. 10 is the surface structure of the matrix sentence. We now need to embed a sentence that has the shape: *wh-witches dance at midnight*. The terminal string in the phrase-structure derivation of this sentence is:

1a. $wh\text{-} + N + Z_2 + Pres + V_i + Tm$

Substituting words from the lexicon gives:

2a. $wh\text{-} + witch + Z_2 + Pres + dance + at\ midnight$

The flip-flop transformation and the morphographemic rules give:

3a. *wh- + witches + dance + at midnight*

We now embed this constituent sentence into the matrix:

11. *those + witches (+ wh- + witches + dance + at midnight) + will + become + hungry*

This string satisfies the requirements of transformation T 4.5, so we may apply it to get the final string:

12. *those + witches + who + dance + at midnight + will + become + hungry*

Removing the plus-signs and applying the appropriate rules of punctuation gives:

13. Those witches who dance at midnight will become hungry.

Derivation of Sentence 4.16.

We shall leave the line-by-line derivation of Sentence 4.16 as an exercise for the reader. The terminal string of the phrase-structure derivation of the matrix sentence is:

1. $Art + N + Z_2 (+S) + Pas + V_t + Art + N + Z_2 (+S)$

Substituting words from the lexicon and applying the flip-flop transformation and the relevant morphographemic rules gives:

2. *the + pterodactyls (+S) + entertained + some + children (+S)*

The first constituent sentence must be *The pterodactyls are in the forest*; the second must be *The children are lonesome*. Underlying these two constituent sentences are the following terminal strings for the phrase-structure derivations:

1a. $Art + N + Z_2 + Pres + be + Loc$
1b. $Art + N + Z_2 + Pres + be + Adj$

Substituting words from the lexicon and applying the flip-flop transformation and the relevant morphographemic rules gives:

2a. *the + pterodactyls + are + in the forest*
2b. *the + children + are + lonesome*

We can now embed these constituents into the matrix:

3. *the + pterodactyls (+ the + pterodactyls + are + in the forest) + entertained + some + children (+ the + children + are + lonesome)*

Because there is identity between the first and second nouns in the matrix sentence and the nouns in the respective constituent sentences, we may apply transformations T 4.6 and T 4.4 to give:

4. *the + pterodactyls + in the forest + entertained + some + lonesome + children*

Finally, removing the plus signs and applying the relevant rules of punctuation gives:

5. The pterodactyls in the forest entertained some lonesome children.

4.7 NOMINALS REVISITED

With the exception of the pronouns, there are no essential differences between those nominals which can occur in the first position of a kernel sentence and those which can occur in the third. Some verbs, as we have noted, must be followed by animate objects just as some verbs must have animate subjects. But these are not restrictions on the kinds of operations that nominals can undergo in these positions.

Earlier in the chapter, we noticed that there were other kinds of nominals besides the common $Det + N + N^{\circ}$. In the following few pages, we will investigate some additional facts about these other kinds of nominals.

As we have already noted, R. B. Lees has given the most exhaustive analysis of English nominalizations. As Lees himself admits in the Preface to the third printing (dated January 1964),[6] the details of his analysis must be revised. But we can assume that the general conclusions of his study are accurate. He gives a number of nominalization transformations, most particularly: (1) **Factive Nominal**, (2) **Action Nominal**, (3) **Agentive Nominal**, (4) **Gerundive Nominal**, and (5) **Infinitival Nominal**. In addition, he discusses various "nominal compounds" such as *girlfriend, madman, arrowhead, gunpowder*, and *St. James Infirmary*. In the following discussion, we shall look at the transformations in some detail, but we shall bring Lees' presentation into greater conformity with recent theoretical advances. Then we shall look cursorily at the nominal compounds.

Factive Nominals.   Lees gives this name to the combination of *that + sentence* constructions which can serve as subjects and objects in certain kinds of sentences:

Sentence 4.17   That she is lovely seems obvious.

Sentence 4.18   John believed that she would marry him.

In analyzing these sentences we need to draw upon the notion of PRO forms. Thus, we can say that the following sentences underline the two factive nominal sentences:

Sentence 4.17a   *SOMETHING* seems obvious. (matrix)

Sentence 4.17b   She is lovely. (constituent)

Sentence 4.18a   John believed *SOMETHING*. (matrix)

Sentence 4.18b   She will marry him. (constituent)

In the derivation of Sentence 4.17a and 4.18a the symbol PRO_N is followed by an optional $(+S)$. The transformation operates in two stages: it first nominalizes the constituent sentence by introducing *that* before $Nom + VP$, and it then deletes the PRO form in the matrix. That is, we begin with:

Sentence 4.17c   *SOMETHING* (She is lovely) seems obvious.

---

[8] Lees, *op. cit.*

We then proceed in two steps:

Sentence 4.17d *SOMETHING* (that she is lovely) seems
obvious.

Sentence 4.17e That she is lovely seems obvious.

But just as there are restrictions on other rules (e.g., on
the selection of singular and plural determiners), so also
are there restrictions on this transformation. In particular,
not all verbs can be preceded by factive nominals. For example, intransitive verbs can only rarely take factive
nominals for subjects:

*That she is lovely may have arrived.

(In contrast, a verb that takes the factive nominal is illustrated in: *That she is lovely may have influenced John.*)
The list of verbs that will take factive nominals for subjects is rather long. Since native speakers of English generally do not confuse these verbs, we shall give only the
three most common types: (1) some form of *to be*; (2) one
of certain copulative verbs; and (3) a verb which must take
an animate object. Thus, we have sentences like:

Sentence 4.19 That this is difficult is unfortunate.

Sentence 4.20 That John will marry her seems certain.

Sentence 4.21 That she would marry him astonishes everyone.

The procedure for deriving Sentence 4.18 is similar to that
for Sentence 4.17:

Sentence 4.18c John believed *SOMETHING* (she will marry
him).

Sentence 4.18d John believed *SOMETHING* (that she will
marry him).

Sentence 4.18e John believed that she would marry him.

Notice that the tense in the constituent sentence generally
agrees with that in the matrix (this is not true in all languages). And as before there are some restrictions on the
kinds of verb that can occur in the matrix. If the wrong

kind of verb is present, then the transformation will not operate. (Many linguists prefer to say that the transformation is "blocked.")

Action Nominals. Where school grammars normally refer to any *verb + ing* combination that is used in some kind of nominal fashion as a **gerund**, Lees quite correctly distinguishes three kinds of constructions. There are simple gerunds which are always count or mass nouns, and there are two additional kinds of gerunds which are always abstract nouns. The regular gerunds are familiar to most teachers:

Sentence 4.22   The dentist put in two new *fillings* today. (count)

Sentence 4.23   The football team took another horrible *beating* this week. (count)

Sentence 4.24   His *writing* was very difficult to read. (mass)

The other two forms, which Lees calls action nominals and gerundive nominals, behave in a significantly different fashion from regular gerunds.

Action nominals have the following characteristics:

1. They function as abstract nouns. (See Sentence 4.25.)
2. They may be preceded by any adjective which can also form an adverb by adding {-ly}. (See Sentence 4.26.)
3. They must be preceded by either the genitive form of a noun (which was the former subject of the verb before it was transformed into an action nominal) or by a determiner other than the zero determiner. (See Sentence 4.27.)

In addition, action nominals which were derived from transitive verbs have another characteristic:

4. If they retain their direct object, then the word *of* must intervene between the nominal and the object. (See Sentence 4.28.)

And there are three constraints:

5. They cannot be preceded by auxiliary verbs.
6. Not all verbs can be transformed into action nominals.
7. They cannot be followed by adverbs of manner.

We can illustrate these statements with the following examples:

Sentence 4.25 John's *singing* could hardly be improved.

Sentence 4.26 John's *magnificent* singing delighted us all.

Sentence 4.27 *The* magnificent singing of "Celeste Aida" was the high point of the evening.

Sentence 4.28 John's *singing of the last few measures* brought the audience to their feet.

The following illustrate the constraints on action nominals:

*Singing of the last few measures brought the audience to their feet. (Action nominals cannot be preceded by the zero article.)

*John's having sung could hardly be improved. (Action nominals cannot be preceded by auxiliary verbs.)

*John's having of a magnificent voice pleases everyone. (The verb *to have* does not form an action nominal.)

*John's singing so well of "Celeste Aida" was the high point of the evening. (Action nominals do not take adverbs of manner.)

The following are characteristics of the transformation that produces action nominals from constituent sentences: (1) deletes all auxiliary verbs; (2) adds a genitive morpheme to the subject (or replaces the subject with some determiner that can precede an abstract noun); (3) adds an {-ing} to the base form of the verb; (4) deletes the {-ly} from all adverbs of manner and places the adjective produced by the deletion in a prenominal position; (5) inserts *of* between the new nominal and the former object if the constituent sentence contains a transitive verb and its object; and (6) deletes the PRO form of the matrix sentence.

Take Sentence 4.27 as an example. The matrix sentence can be represented as follows:

Sentence 4.27a *SOMETHING* (+S) was the high point of the evening.

The constituent sentence then replaces the optional *S*:

Sentence 4.27b *SOMETHING* (John sings "Celeste Aida" magnificently) was the high point of the evening.

Steps (1) through (5) of the transformation produce:

Sentence 4.27c *SOMETHING* (The magnificent singing of "Celeste Aida") was the high point of the evening.

And the final step deletes the PRO form. All action nominals are produced by a similar transformation.

Agentive Nominals. This transformation produces names for those agents who perform particular actions. Agentive nominals, therefore, are always count nouns. All of the transitive and intransitive verbs that take animate subjects can be transformed into agentive nominals. As is the case with action nominals, the object of a transformed transitive verb can be retained but must be separated from the nominal by the word *of*, and any adverbials of manner present in the constituent sentence must be changed to prenominal adjectives.

Thus, the sentence

Sentence 4.29 John is a singer of songs

comes from:

Sentence 4.29a John is *SOMEONE* (+S). (matrix)
Sentence 4.29b *SOMEONE* sings songs. (constituent)
Sentence 4.29c John is *SOMEONE* (*SOMEONE* sings songs). (new matrix)
Sentence 4.29 John is a singer of songs.

When the previous object is animate, it can precede the agentive nominal as a genitive. Thus we get:

Sentence 4.30a George is *SOMEONE* (+S). (matrix)

Sentence 4.30b   *SOMEONE* admires Marge. (constituent)
Sentence 4.30c   George is *SOMEONE* (*SOMEONE* admires Marge). (new matrix)
Sentence 4.30d   George is the admirer of Marge. (agentive transformation)
Sentence 4.30e   George is Marge's admirer. (stylistic variation)

The transformation attaches the agentive morpheme {-er} onto the base form of the verb. There are, however, several allomorphs of this morpheme as well as several alternative forms that generally take precedent over a regular agentive nominal:

Sentence 4.31a   Gerry is *SOMEONE*. (matrix)
Sentence 4.31b   *SOMEONE* acts well. (constituent)
Sentence 4.31c   Gerry is a good act*or*. (allomorphic variant)
Sentence 4.32a   Frank is *SOMEONE*. (matrix)
Sentence 4.32b   *SOMEONE* speaks for the group. (constituent)
Sentence 4.32c   Frank is the speaker for the group. (regular agentive)
Sentence 4.32d   Frank is the spokesman for the group. (alternative form)

Gerundive Nominals.   Gerundive nominals differ from both regular gerunds and action nominals. They have the following characteristics:

1. They cannot be preceded by the adjective form of manner adverbials. (See Sentence 4.33.)
2. They retain the perfect-tense auxiliary (i.e., the verb *to have*) when they are transformed. (See Sentence 4.33.)
3. They can be modified by any adverb that modifies the verb in the constituent sentence. (See Sentence 4.34.)
4. The genitive which precedes the nominal cannot be replaced by any other form of determiner (except the zero article).
5. All verbs can form gerundive nominals. (See Sentence 4.35.)

The following sentences illustrate these characteristics:

Sentence 4.33   John's having sung well in many concerts
is evidence of his ability.

But the sentence below is not acceptable:

*John's good having sung in many concerts is evidence of
his ability.

As Sentence 4.33 suggests, the perfect-tense auxiliary in
the constituent sentence—in this case, Sentence 4.33a:
John has *sung well in many concerts*—is carried into the
gerundive nominal by the transformation.

Sentence 4.34   John's having sung frequently and magnificently, both here and abroad, is evidence of his ability.

The following sentence demonstrates a constraint:

*The having sung well is evidence of his ability. (Only
genitives or the zero article can precede a gerundive nominal.)

Sentence 4.35   Having a good voice is a gift bestowed on few.

But a corresponding action nominal is not acceptable:

*"Having of a good voice is a gift bestowed on few"

Notice that when a transitive verb is transformed into
a gerundive nominal, the former object is not separated
from the nominal by the word *of*.

Infinitival Nominals. Lees gives three kinds of infinitival nominals: (1) those occurring as subject of a copulative sentence; (2) those that are objects of a restricted class
of verbs; and (3) those that occur in adverbials of purpose
(or "use") following the word *for*. In each case, the word
for serves to mark the occurrence of the infinitival nominal. Thus we have:

Sentence 4.36   For me to study hard is unusual.

(The sentence is derived from the constituent: *I study
hard*.)

Sentence 4.37 My counselor pleaded for me to study hard.

Sentence 4.38 I bought this corsage for you to wear.

The last sentence is derived from:

Sentence 4.38a I bought this corsage for *SOMETHING* (you wear the corsage).

The subjects of infinitival nominals may be deleted, although in doing so we must be particularly careful to avoid ambiguity. That is, we can say:

Sentence 4.38b I bought this corsage to wear.

In this case, we have deleted the former subject of the embedded sentence but, in contrast with Sentence 4.38, we no longer know the "person" (i.e., *I, you, he, she, we, they*) of the subject. A larger context, of course, may provide sufficient information so that we are able to determine the former subject precisely:

Sentence 4.38c I bought this corsage for *SOMETHING* (you treasure the corsage) and for *SOMETHING* (you wear the corsage).

In this case, we can easily delete the subject of the second embedded sentence to give:

Sentence 4.38d I bought this corsage for you to treasure and to wear.

There are many subtleties connected with the formation of infinitival nominals that have not yet been completely worked out. For example, their behavior in a sentence is different from that of infinitives in such sentences as *He likes to eat.* Some investigations currently under way should shed some light on these differences.

Nominal Compounds. Probably some of Lees' analysis of compound nominals needs to be re-evaluated in terms of recent advances in the study of English. But it does seem certain that rules of compound formation, similar to the transformational rules which produce nominalizations, can be formulated. These rules will certainly generate the various kinds of nominal compounds that Lees gives. By way of example, we can list the following types:

1. Subject-Predicate
2. Subject-Verb
3. Verb-Prepositional Object

The first type of compound is formed from sentences such as:

Sentence 4.39   *The boy is a friend.* $\longrightarrow$ *boyfriend.*
Sentence 4.40   *The dog is a hound.* $\longrightarrow$ *hounddog.*

The second type is formed from sentences such as:

Sentence 4.41   *The toes twinkle.* $\longrightarrow$ *twinkletoes.*
Sentence 4.42   *The sun shines.* $\longrightarrow$ *sunshine.*

And the third type is formed from:

Sentence 4.43   *This fountain is for drinking.* $\longrightarrow$ *drinking fountain.*
Sentence 4.44   *This basket is for waste.* $\longrightarrow$ *waste basket.*

Lees' pioneering study made no attempt to account for the variety of restrictions that must be imposed on transformational rules of this type. Nonetheless, he does indicate the variety of possibilities available to speakers of a language.

4.8   SUMMARY

This chapter has been concerned with five primary topics:

1. The determiner system
2. Kinds of nouns
3. Adjectives (a noun modifier which precedes the noun)
4. Nouns in apposition, relative clauses, locative adverbs
5. Nominalization transformations

We saw that the determiner system, though complex, seldom causes problems for native speakers of English. We investigated the traditional varieties of nouns and added the notion of count nouns. We saw how adjectives are introduced into a prenominal position by embedding a constituent sentence into a matrix sentence. And we noticed the close connection among the various kinds of postnominal modifiers as well as the connection between them and adjectives.

In this discussion we introduced several new rules into the model grammar. The most important of these is the one that makes the grammar recursive by incorporating an optional symbol *S* in the expansion of *Nom*. This recursive *S* rule makes the number of possible sentences in the language infinite and also enables us to introduce many modifiers into basic kernel sentences. We also established the notion of PRO forms and investigated the relation between these forms and the rule of recoverability for transformational deletions. We touched briefly upon pronouns, including the reflexives and intensifiers. And, finally, we looked at some of the ways of making new nominals. Now we are ready to look at the verb system of English.

Discussion

1. Compare the determiner system of Modern English with the determiner system of Old English or of some foreign language. Are the determiner systems of highly inflected Indo-European languages as complex as the determiner system of English? Why? What features distinguish the determiners, as a class, from adjectives? What are some of the restrictions on the occurrence of determiners, in addition to those given in the text (e.g., some prearticles can co-occur with other prearticles—*just both boys*—while others cannot—*both only boys*)?

2. Why is the term count noun more accurate than the term concrete noun? Mass nouns and abstract nouns generally function in identical ways (i.e., syntactically). What are the advantages of creating two separate categories for these kinds of nouns? Besides those listed in the text, what other features (e.g., animate, inanimate) can nouns have? What are some of the ways in which features overlap? (For example, *army* is both a mass and an animate noun.)

3. List the way or ways in which the following are similar: (1) nouns in apposition, (2) relative clauses, and (3) postnominal locative adverbs. In what ways are they similar to prenominal adjectives? Does the "traditional school-grammar" definition of adverb account for the occurrence of postnominal locative adverbs? What does this suggest about such definitions? Compare some of the other traditional definitions to see if they are complete.

4. Consult several dictionaries for a definition of "recursiveness." How do these definitions apply to grammar? How does the property of recursiveness function to make English infinite? What are some of the essential differences between (1) an infinite number of sentences, and (2) an infinitely long sentence? In what way or ways is simple arithmetic recursive?

5. Define the differences that exist among the following kinds of nominals: (1) factive, (2) action, (3) agentive, (4) gerundive, and (5) infinitival. What are the differences between this group of nominals, as a class, and the group of nominal compounds (such as *girlfriend* or *airplane*)? What does this comparison suggest about the ways in which we create new words in English?

Exercises

1. Identify the kinds of determiners in the following sentences:

    a. All three of those men are just my type.
    b. You may take both of the last two pieces of his pie.
    c. I bought the last two copies of both of those books.

2. List all of the features for each of the nouns in the following sentences:

    a. Churchill was a man among men.
    b. This coffee doesn't taste like coffee at all.
    c. A group of boys can cause a peck of trouble.

3. Identify the kinds of nominalizations that occur in each of the following sentences:

    a. I know that he is a watchmaker.
    b. She finds his constant questioning of her motives very annoying.
    c. Is it not passing brave to be a king?
    d. They say that many people object to your mixing gunpowder with ice cream.

4. Derive the matrix sentence and the two constituent sentences of Sentence 4.16. Construct a branching tree diagram for the matrix sentence.

5. Identify the transformations that have been applied to produce the following sentences (all of which can be derived from the third model grammar).

    a. Those monsters there may frighten the happy children.
    b. Any man who sleeps in that forest will become angry.
    c. The monster, an angry dragon, devoured the lonesome witch.
    d. The happy aardvark will see the children today.

⟨5⟩

The Verb

For there be women fair as she
Whose nouns and verbs do more agree.
BRET HARTE, "Mrs. Judge Jenkins"

As Bret Harte notes rather mournfully, we sometimes base social opinions on a speaker's ability to control his — or her — verbs. No grammatical error is more easily recognized by an English teacher or the general public. No teacher fails to point out faulty agreement to wayward students. But people still make errors in agreement and tense. Why?

The answer isn't hard to find. As teachers we are generally guilty of assuming that the English verb is similar to the Latin verb. We spend useless hours in futile conjugation, and we overlook the unique — and even elegant — properties of the English verb system.

But the tradition of Latin methods is so deep in English pedagogy that we can best begin by making a brief comparison of the verbs in both languages.

Take, for example, a regular Latin verb of the third conjugation: *mittere*, "to send." In the first-person singular of the active voice, indicative mood, there are the following forms:

mitto:	I send, I am sending, I do send
mittebam:	I was sending, I sent
mittam:	I shall send
misi:	I sent, I have sent

118

| *miseram:* | I had sent |
| *misero:* | I shall have sent |

Since there are five other persons (*thou; he, she, it; we; you; they*), the active indicative has a total of thirty-six different forms. There are four tenses, with six persons each, in the active subjunctive for a total of twenty-four additional forms. There are two singular and three plural forms for the active imperative. And if we include the passive indicative, passive subjunctive, and passive imperative, as well as all the participles, we will have a total of 156 forms. *And this does not include the auxiliary verb forms.* In sharp contrast, the regular English verb has only four forms (we again omit the auxiliary verb as we did in compiling the list of Latin forms). The irregular English verb (except for the verb *to be*) has no more than five forms, and the verb *to be* has eight:

call, calls, called, calling (regular English verb)
sing, sings, sang, sung, singing (irregular English verb)
be, am, is, are, was, were, been, being

What is equally important is that in many cases a single form of a Latin verb may be translated in two or three ways in English. For example, *mitto* is "I send, I am sending, I do send." And *misi* is "I sent, I have sent."

These facts indicate that any description of the English verb system that is based on the model of Latin or any other highly inflected language is bound to be confusing and may be misleading. In other words, we must describe the English verb in terms of its own unique features. On the other hand, this does not mean that we must discard all of the Latin terms. English obviously has a present and a past; it has participles and gerunds; it has infinitives and auxiliaries. But the form of each of these is unique to English.

5.1   THE MAIN VERB

As we have seen in Chapter 2, the main verb in an English sentence generally fits into one of four classes: (1) *to be*, (2) intransitive, (3) transitive, and (4) copulative. Some verbs may belong to more than one class, and some classes have subclasses that contain verbs having most but not all of the features of the main class. These facts underlie the following discussion of verbs. Only enough detail is included in the discussion, however, to indicate the general nature and broad outlines of a complete scientific description of the English verb system. For the purposes of most pedagogical grammars, the distinctions made in a scientific grammar are not always relevant.[1]

In this chapter, we shall not elaborate on those sentences in which the verb *to be* is used as a main verb, that is, on sentences of the form:

$$Nom + be + Pred + Adv$$

In Chapter 6, however, we shall discuss some of the restrictions on the elements that can appear in the *Pred* as well as some of the restrictions on the occurrence of certain adverbs following the verb *to be*.

Intransitive Verbs.   As a class, intransitive verbs cannot be followed by nominals or adjectives in the third position. In other words, the third position in a sentence containing an intransitive verb is empty. But not all intransitive verbs are alike. In particular, some intransitive verbs must be followed by adverbs of location (e.g., *The baby is lying in the bed*), and some by adverbs of motion (e.g., *The thief is sneaking away*). Most intransitive verbs, however, can occur with or without adverbs (e.g., *come, shiver, sleep, disappear*).

---

[1] For example, linguists constructing a scientific grammar of English must distinguish those transitive verbs which take animate (generally "human") subjects (such as *admire* and *find*) from those which take animate objects (such as *terrify* and *astonish*). They must also distinguish transitive verbs that can be followed by a human object plus an infinitive (such as *We selected Gerry to go* and *He persuaded Joan to accompany him*) from those that can be followed by a human object plus a present participle (such as *They found the professor fishing* and *They caught the student sleeping*). Such subtleties, though obviously real, are beyond the scope of this text.

The following sentences all contain intransitive verbs:

Sentence 5.1   George ran quickly.
Sentence 5.2   Howard slept here.
Sentence 5.3   Judith may come soon.

Transitive Verbs.   Transitive verbs are somewhat more complicated than intransitive verbs. All transitive verbs can be followed by nominals in the third position. This nominal is known as the **direct object**. But some transitive verbs can be followed by both a direct object and an indirect object. Some sentences containing particular kinds of transitive verbs cannot be transformed to form a passive-voice sentence. And still other kinds of transitive verbs can be followed by both an object and a construction traditionally called the **objective complement**. We can discuss each of these broad categories in turn.

Except for some subtle restrictions (such as those indicated in Footnote 1), regular transitive verbs are remarkably free. They are followed, in position three, by nominals, and in position four, by nearly every kind of adverb (*Man, Loc, Tm, Rsn,* and so on).

Sentence 5.4   Joe read the role admirably.
Sentence 5.5   The chairman rode his motorcycle in the rain.
Sentence 5.6   Betty bought a hat today.
Sentence 5.7   The barber gave a party for his friends.

Most transitive verbs, however, cannot be followed by both a direct and indirect object. For example, most verbs that require animate objects (such as *surprise* and *please*) cannot take indirect objects. That is, we can say:

Sentence 5.8   Simone surprised her husband.
Sentence 5.9   The monster terrified the children.

But we cannot say:

*Simone surprised her husband to him.
*The monster terrified them the children.

The second subclass of transitive verbs, generally called **middle verbs** (V_{mid}), cannot be transformed to form a passive sentence. The italicized words in the following sentences are typical middle verbs:

Sentence 5.10   This book *weighs* five pounds.
Sentence 5.11   The china *costs* eight dollars.
Sentence 5.12   Ed *has* a good library.
Sentence 5.13   The beard *suits* his personality.

There are no corresponding passives for these sentences:

*Five pounds are weighed by the book.
*Eight dollars are cost by the china.
*A good library is had by Ed.
*His personality is suited by the beard.

There is another distinction between regular transitive verbs and middle verbs: the former, as Lees has noted,[2] can be transformed into action nominals with *of* while the latter cannot. That is, there are nominals of the form:

Sentence 5.14   Joe's reading of the role (delighted the audience).

But there are no nominals of the form:

*The book's weighing of five pounds . . .

Interestingly, many of the middle verbs cannot be followed by adverbs of manner. Thus, we cannot say: *Ed has a good library quickly*. But this is not a consistent feature of all middle verbs.

The third subclass of transitive verbs includes those that can be followed by both a direct object and an objective complement. In particular, it includes verbs like those in the following sentences:

Sentence 5.15   We elected John president.
Sentence 5.16   They licked the platter clean.

---

[2] Lees, *Grammar of English Nominalizations*, p. 8.

Sentences of this type are probably derived by embedding a constituent sentence of the type $Nom + be + Pred$ after the noun that is the direct object. Thus, at some point in the derivation of Sentence 5.15, we would have a string such as:

$$Nom + Pas + V_{oc} + Nom (+S)$$

where V_{oc} represents a transitive verb which can (or must) be followed by a direct object and an objective complement. Later in the derivation we might have a string such as the following:

$$We + elected + John (+ John + is + president)$$

An obligatory transformation would then delete both the repeated nominal and the verb to give the required sentence.

Copulative Verbs.   Copulative verbs can also be divided into several subclasses. In our earlier analysis and in the three model grammars, we have indicated that copulative verbs are followed only by adjectives. This, of course, is an oversimplification. All copulative verbs can be followed by adjectives, but some can also be followed by nominals, and at least two can be followed by a locative adverb (and these verbs thus resemble the verb *to be*). A close analysis of English reveals the following general types of copulative verbs:

1. Verbs of the senses (V_s): *feel, smell, taste,* and so on.
2. Verbs of appearance (V_{ap}): *appear, look, seem,* and so on.
3. Verbs of action (V_{ac}): *grow, turn,* and so on.
4. *become*
5. *stay* and *remain*

Copulative verbs of the senses can only be followed by adjectives:

Sentence 5.17   The steak tastes delicious.
Sentence 5.18   The warm sun feels good.

The same verbs can also be used as transitive verbs, in which case they are followed by direct objects:

> Sentence 5.19   Bob tasted the steak.
> Sentence 5.20   I felt the sun on my arm.

Verbs of appearance (in American English) cannot be followed by nominals. They differ from verbs of sensation because they can take abstract nouns for subjects. They can also be followed by the infinitive *to be*. For example:

> Sentence 5.21   His happiness seems to be complete.
> Sentence 5.22   John appears to be sad.

The third subclass of copulative verbs, verbs of action or activity, can be followed by adverbs of manner, whereas the first two subclasses cannot be followed by such adverbs. Thus, we have:

> Sentence 5.23   George grew tall gradually.
> Sentence 5.24   The boy turned blue slowly.

But we cannot have:

> *The steak tastes delicious gradually.
> *John appears sad slowly.

Last, we can treat *become* and *stay* and *remain* as special sub-classes of copulative verbs. Like copulative verbs of activity, *become* can be followed by adverbs of manner; unlike most of them, however, it easily takes nominals in the third position. Thus, we can say:

> Sentence 5.25   Marvin became a psychologist.
> Sentence 5.26   Tilly became a teacher unexpectedly.

But we cannot say:

> *George grew a psychologist.
> *The boy turned a teacher unexpectedly.[3]

---

[3] If *turn* is understood here in the transitive sense of "rotate," then this sentence, though bizarre, is not ungrammatical.

The verbs *stay* and *remain*, when used as copulative verbs, seem to share all the properties of the verb *to be*. That is, they can be followed by nominals, adjectives, and locatives:

Sentence 5.27   John stayed president for one year.

Sentence 5.28   John stayed happy all day.

Sentence 5.29   John stayed in the house.

Verbs, Prepositions, and Particles. Most school grammars ignore the fact that English, like other Germanic languages, has verbs which consist of two or more words. In fact, it has two distinct kinds of these verbs. The first kind includes such verbs as:

look at	speak to	think about
belong to	wait for	seek after

As the examples indicate, the construction consists of a verb plus a preposition $(Vb + P)$. These verbs function in the language as a subclass of transitive verbs (V_t):

Sentence 5.30   Some expert should look at the problem more closely.

Sentence 5.31   The principal should speak to that boy more often.

These sentences contain an occurrence of $V_t + Nom$ (where the V_t is $Vb + P$), rather than an occurrence of V_i + prepositional phrase. We can see this most easily by transforming the sentence into the passive voice:

Sentence 5.30a   The problem should be looked at more closely (by some expert).

Sentence 5.31a   That boy should be spoken to more often (by the principal).

In each case, the preposition remains with the verb rather than moving with the nominal. In other words, the nominals (*the problem* and *that boy*) are the direct objects of the verbs (*look at* and *speak to*), rather than the objects of a preposition.

There is a related construction in the language which includes such verbs as:

turn on	bring in	shut off
give up	wear out	break down

Linguists designate these constructions as verb-plus-particle (*Vb* + *Prt*); they differ from the verb-plus-preposition construction since the particle is movable:

Sentence 5.32a Polly has turned on the light.

Sentence 5.32b Polly has turned the light on.

Sentence 5.33a The policeman brought in the criminal.

Sentence 5.33b The policeman brought the criminal in.

As the examples indicate, the particle can precede or follow the nominal that is the direct object of the verb. There is a significant exception to this generalization: when the direct object is a pronoun, then the particle *must* follow:

Sentence 5.32c Polly has turned it on.

Sentence 5.33c The policeman brought him in.

These sentences can also be transformed into the passive:

Sentence 5.32d The light has been turned on (by Polly).

Sentence 5.33d The criminal was brought in (by the policeman).

The preposition (in the verb-plus-preposition construction) and the particle must both be distinguished, first, from prepositions that are not combined with verbs, and second, from those adverbs that are spelled the same way that certain prepositions are. Consider the words that are italicized in the following sentences:

Sentence 5.34 We need not think *about* this question until tomorrow.

Sentence 5.35 I have already shut *off* the faucet.

Sentence 5.36 That man lives *on* the mountain.

Sentence 5.37 He was afraid to jump *down*.

In Sentence 5.34 *about* is the preposition in the verb-plus-preposition construction *think about*. The direct object of the *Vb + P* is *this question*. The preposition cannot be moved to a position following the direct object, but the sentence can be transformed into a passive:

Sentence 5.34a This question need not be thought about (by us) until tomorrow.

In Sentence 5.35 *off* is the particle in the verb-plus-particle construction *shut off*. The direct object of the *Vb + Prt* is *the faucet*. The particle can be moved to a position following the direct object, and the sentence can also be transformed into a passive:

Sentence 5.35a I have already shut the faucet off.
Sentence 5.35b The faucet has already been shut off (by me).

In Sentence 5.36 *on* is a regular preposition that introduces an adverbial prepositional phrase of location (*Loc*): *on the mountain*. The preposition cannot be moved to a position following the nominal. In Sentence 5.37 *down* is an adverb of location (*Loc*) and, as such, can be contrasted with the particle *down* in such constructions as *We broke down the door* and *We broke the door down*. That is, in Sentence 5.37, the adverb *down* is not a part of the verb *jump* nor is it a part of a prepositional phrase.

One final set of examples should clarify the matter. Each of the following sentences is ambiguous; that is, each sentence has two meanings and two possible derivations:

Sentence 5.38 Allen often fights with his friends.
Sentence 5.39 Charles has worn his new sweater out.

Sentence 5.38 is ambiguous in two ways: (1) *with* could be a part of the verb (*Vb + P*), in which case *his friends* would be the direct object and the sentence could be interpreted to mean that "Allen is antagonistic toward his friends"; and (2) *with* could be a part of a prepositional phrase known technically as a **concomitave adverbial phrase**[4] in

---

[4] See Chapter 6 for a discussion of this term.

which case the sentence could mean that "Allen and his friends are often on the same side and, together, they fight a common enemy." In both interpretations *with* is a preposition, but in the first case, the preposition is part of the verb, and in the second case, the preposition is part of an adverbial prepositional phrase. Sentence 5.39 is also ambiguous since (1) *out* could be a particle and a part of the verb *wear out* ("Charles has worn out his sweater"); and (2) *out* could be an adverb of location meaning "outside." The ambiguities can be explained only if we distinguish carefully among (1) regular prepositions, (2) combinations of verb-plus-preposition ($Vb + P$), (3) combinations of verb-plus-particle ($Vb + Prt$), and (4) adverbs that are spelled the same way that certain prepositions are. The failure to make these distinctions is largely responsible for the confusion about "not ending a sentence with a preposition." Such strictures have led to a needless self-consciousness on the part of many speakers and have undoubtedly robbed the language of at least part of its flexibility.

These distinctions regarding the various kinds of verbs must all be incorporated in a scientific grammar of English and, when necessary, can be incorporated in a pedagogical grammar. There are also distinctions that relate to the auxiliary verb system of English.

5.2 AUXILIARY VERBS

In contrast to Latin and other highly inflected languages, any single English verb (that is, any verb without auxiliaries) must be in one of two tenses: **present** or **past**. For example, with the verbs *to call* and *to walk*, we may say:

$$\left.\begin{array}{l} \text{I} \\ \text{you} \\ \text{we} \\ \text{they} \end{array}\right\} \left\{\begin{array}{l} \text{call} \\ \text{walk} \end{array}\right. \qquad \left.\begin{array}{l} \text{he} \\ \text{she} \\ \text{it} \end{array}\right\} \left\{\begin{array}{l} \text{calls} \\ \text{walks} \end{array}\right.$$

$$
\left.\begin{array}{l}
\text{I} \\
\text{you} \\
\text{he, she, it} \\
\text{we} \\
\text{they}
\end{array}\right\} \quad \left\{\begin{array}{l}
\text{called} \\
\text{walked}
\end{array}\right.
$$

To form all other tenses in English, we must use a combination of auxiliary and main verbs.

There are three main types of auxiliaries in English, and they function with strict regularity. We have already briefly noted the first type of auxiliary: the modal. We can restrict the modals to four which have both a present and past form (*can, may, shall, will*) and one which has only a present form (*must*). Since English is a flexible and changing language, it is not surprising to discover that we use many other verbs as if they were modals (*need* and *dare* bear the strongest resemblance to the regular modals), but we shall not treat these in detail in this text.[5] The modals have two distinct features: in the third-person singular form of the present tense, they do not have the bound morpheme {-*s*}, which is a distinguishing characteristic of all other verbs; and when the main verb directly follows the modal, then neither the modal nor the main verb carries a bound morpheme except for the *Tn* marker on the auxiliary. In addition, there is no infinitive form of a true modal verb. And finally, when the modal is used as an auxiliary, it always precedes all the other auxiliaries.

There are two other auxiliaries besides the modals: *to have* and *to be*. When *have* is used as an auxiliary, the verb that follows is invariably in the past participle form. Thus, we have:

Sentence 5.40   Ronnie has eaten the lobster.

Sentence 5.41   Valerie has been typing all day.

---

[5] These irregular modals occur easily in negative sentences: *I cannot go, I will not go, I dare not go,* and *I need not go*. But not all American dialects have the positive forms of the last two sentences: *I dare go* and *I need go*.

The verbs *eaten* and *been*, both of which immediately follow *has*, are past participles. This rule, it is worth repeating, is invariable in English.

When *be* is used as an auxiliary in any sentence in the active voice, the verb that follows (and it will always be the main verb) is invariably in the present participle form. (We shall treat the verb *to be* used as an auxiliary in passive sentences in Chapter 7.) Thus, we have:

Sentence 5.42   Al was delivering a lecture.
Sentence 5.43   Jo is painting the chairs.

In these examples, both *delivering* and *painting* are present participles.

We can now expand the phrase-structure rule for auxiliaries:

PS 5.5 $Aux \longrightarrow Tn$ (*Modal*) (*have* + *en*) (*be* + *ing*)

Briefly, this rule says that we must choose the tense morpheme and we may choose one or more of the auxiliaries. The auxiliaries invariably retain the order shown. That is, the modal is always the first auxiliary when it occurs with others; *have* follows the modal and precedes the verb *to be* if either or both occur; and *be* is always the last auxiliary when it is used with at least one other. The following sentences illustrate these facts:

Sentence 5.44   The boy will run. (modal only)
Sentence 5.45   The boy will have run. (modal and *have*)
Sentence 5.46   The boy will be running. (modal and *be*)
Sentence 5.47   The boy will have been running. (modal, *have*, and *be*)
Sentence 5.48   The boy has run. (*have* only)
Sentence 5.49   The boy has been running. (*have* and *be*)
Sentence 5.50   The boy is running (*be* only).

But the phrase-structure rule for auxiliaries shows even more. Notice that we must choose the morpheme {*Tn*}. In a later phrase-structure rule, we must rewrite {*Tn*} as either {*Pres*} or {*Pas*}. The affix transformation (the flip-flop) then automatically attaches the correct tense morpheme *to the first verb in the verbal phrase.* In the examples above, the first verb in each of the verbal phrases is in the present tense, indicating that we choose the morpheme {*Pres*} in deriving these sentences. If we had chosen {*Pas*} we would have gotten:

Sentence 5.44a   The boy would run.
Sentence 5.45a   The boy would have run.
Sentence 5.46a   The boy would be running.
Sentence 5.47a   The boy would have been running.
Sentence 5.48a   The boy had run.
Sentence 5.49a   The boy had been running.
Sentence 5.50a   The boy was running.

On the other hand, if we had not chosen any of the parenthesized elements, that is, if we had chosen only the morpheme {*Tn*}, then we would not have any auxiliary verbs and the main verb would be in either the simple present or the simple past form:

Sentence 5.51   The boy runs.
Sentence 5.51a   The boy ran.

In contrast, then, to the long conjugations required for verbs in a highly inflected language like Latin, we can give one simple formula for all sixteen active tenses in English:

Tn (Modal) (have + en) (be + ing) MV

This formula, perhaps more than any other, shows the advantages of transformational grammar over all others.

5.3   YES/NO QUESTIONS AND PREVERBS

The implications of the auxiliary rule go even deeper into the language. Consider Sentence 5.44–Sentence 5.50, all of which contain auxiliary verbs. Any one of these can be transformed into a yes/no question by simply moving the auxiliary verb (or the first auxiliary, when there is more than one) to the first position in the sentence. Thus, selecting at random, we have:

Sentence 5.44b Will the boy run?
Sentence 5.46b Will the boy be running?
Sentence 5.49b Has the boy been running?
Sentence 5.50b Was the boy running?

But, if there are no auxiliary verbs, we cannot move the main verb; that is, in Modern English there are no sentences of the form:

*Runs the boy?
*Ran the boy?

Instead, we must utilize the present or past form of the special auxiliary verb *to do*:

Sentence 5.51b Does the boy run?
Sentence 5.51c Did the boy run?

A similar condition prevails when we introduce the negative morpheme {*Ng*} into a sentence. When an auxiliary verb is present, we may add the word *not* after the auxiliary (or after the first auxiliary if there is more than one). Thus:

Sentence 5.44c The boy will not run.
Sentence 5.46c The boy will not be running.
Sentence 5.49c The boy hasn't been running.
Sentence 5.50c The boy wasn't running.

But the negative morpheme generally cannot be attached to a main verb. There are no sentences of the form:

*The boy runs not.
*The boy not runs.

As before, we must add the present or past form of the special auxiliary *to do*.

Sentence 5.51d   The boy doesn't run.
Sentence 5.51e   The boy didn't run.

There is one interesting exception to the rule that we must use some form of *to do* in yes/no questions and negative sentences when there is no auxiliary verb. It is not necessary to use *to do* in such cases when the main verb is also one that can be used as an auxiliary; that is, when the main verb is some form of *have* or *be*. Thus we can have:

Sentence 5.52a   Bill is happy.
Sentence 5.52b   Is Bill happy?
Sentence 5.52c   Bill isn't happy.
Sentence 5.53a   Ed has a cold.
Sentence 5.53b   Has Ed a cold?
Sentence 5.53c   Ed hasn't a cold.

All this can be incorporated into our model grammar by including an obligatory *do* transformation which correctly inserts the verb *to do* into yes/no questions and negative sentences that do not otherwise contain auxiliaries. We can even formulate the rule so that it takes care of one oddity. When *have* is used as a main verb, we can also, optionally, have some form of the verb *to do*; when *be* is used as a main verb, however, we can never have a form of *to do* in the indicative mood. Thus we cannot have:

*Bill does be happy.
*Does Bill be happy?
*Bill doesn't be happy.

Sentence 5.53d   Ed does have a cold.
Sentence 5.53e   Does Ed have a cold?
Sentence 5.53f   Ed doesn't have a cold.

The fact that *to do* does not occur when *to be* is used as a main verb in indicative sentences accounts, in part, for the fact that we separated sentences with *to be* from all other sentences in Chapter 2.[6]

---

[6] Yes/no questions are discussed more fully in Chapter 7.

Two further facts emerge from this discussion. We can consider *to do* (when used as an obligatory auxiliary) to be a PRO form of the verb. And second, we want to incorporate negatives in the phrase-structure rules. But before writing a rule for incorporating the {*Ng*} morpheme, we must look at some additional sentences:

Sentence 5.54   Fran often has won musical prizes.
Sentence 5.55   Bob has seldom won such prizes.
Sentence 5.56   They always go to Michigan in the summer.
Sentence 5.57   They have never given dull parties.

As these sentences indicate, there are some words (such as *often, seldom, always, never*) which can also occur before the main verb, but they cannot always co-occur with the word *not*. Thus, there are no sentences of the form:

*Bob has not seldom won such prizes.
*They haven't never given dull parties.

As these examples suggest, there is a class of words, which linguists call **preverbs** (*Prev*) that may, in the surface structure, be positive or negative. These preverbs can occur before main verbs directly (*George often reads* or *George seldom reads*), or as part of the auxiliary verb phrase.

The easiest place to introduce all these words into the phrase-structure grammar is in PS rule No. 2, immediately before the symbol for the auxiliary construction. That is:

PS 5.2 $VP \longrightarrow (Prev) \, Aux + MV$

Later in a scientific grammar, we must introduce some rule for rewriting the combination of the negative morpheme {*Ng*} and the preverb. As we shall see in Chapter 6, the negative morpheme is introduced as a presentence element, just as the interrogative morpheme {*Q*} and the emphatic morpheme {*Emph*} are introduced.[7] For the pur-

---

[7] This rule has not yet been completely worked out. In particular, we need to write transformations that change *not ever* to *never* and perhaps *not often* to *rarely*. But the other negative preverbs, such as *hardly*, pose problems that are not yet solved. In a scientific grammar we also need a rule that positions the preverb behind the first auxiliary, if one or more auxiliaries occur.

poses of the fourth model grammar, however, we shall
ignore the *Prev* in PS rule No. 5.2.

5.4   FOURTH MODEL GRAMMAR

We are now ready to incorporate some of the facts discussed in this chapter into a model grammar. As before, not
all of the restrictions are rigorously listed. But the grammar
does include restrictions for those rules which are frequently violated by native speakers of English.[8]

This model grammar also removes the earlier restriction on using the affix (flip-flop) transformation only once;
it does so by introducing a new notion – and a new transformation – that of word boundary. This notion requires
some explanation.

Linguists use the symbol # – called a **double cross** – to
mark both the beginning and end of a sentence, and the
beginning and end of a word. In listening to someone speak,
we can obviously recognize these features, and in writing,
we take note of the features by separating words on the
page and by beginning sentences with a capital letter and
ending them with a period. But these conventions – separation of words, capitalization, and punctuation marks – are
a very recent development in language. In early manuscripts of Old English, for example, many words are run
together. When the author of one of the manuscripts came
to the end of a line, he broke the word anywhere and started
on the next line. And capital letters were relatively unknown. In short, separation of words, capitalization, and
punctuation are attempts on the part of printers and type-
setters to indicate certain features of language that cannot be represented directly in spelling. Linguists, for their
own purposes, have developed an analogous but somewhat
more precise system for indicating the same kinds of fea-

---

[8] Persons who violate these rules (e.g., rules of agreement) probably
grew up speaking a dialect other than the socially acceptable one. Only
rarely do speakers completely lose their original dialects, but most speakers can master two dialects with proper instruction.

tures. The double cross (sometimes also called a **boundary juncture**) is one symbol from the linguistic system.

The initial string of the grammar, then, which we gave simply as S in Chapter 2, should actually be written $\#S\#$. The first double cross in this string indicates the initial boundary of the symbol S; the second double cross indicates the final boundary. Consequently, every line in a derivation should be preceded and followed by the double-cross symbol. (In practice, most linguists show the boundary symbols on the initial and terminal strings only, and this space-saving convention will be adopted in this text.)

The double-cross symbol is actually a morpheme; we can frequently detect its presence in an indicative sentence by the fact that the voice rises slightly at the end and then drops off to a level lower than the starting level of the sentence:

Sentence 5.58   Gertrude has gone to the $s^{ea}sh_{o}r_{e}$.

And since it is a morpheme, it can be indicated in a branching tree:

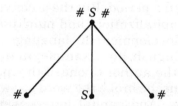

Figure 5.1   Sentence boundaries.

We should note that the S which is optionally embedded in a sentence after any nominal does *not* contain the double-cross morphemes, since it is never an independent sentence but only a means of adding words, phrases, and clauses to a matrix sentence.

The same symbol is used also to indicate the beginning

and end of a word, and also to separate one word from another. To take an earlier example:

> *# un + gentle + man + li + ness #*

Among other things, the absence of a double cross immediately before and after *gentle* indicates that, *in this instance, gentle* is *not* a word but rather a free morpheme to which other morphemes are attached.

Since the items contained between a pair of double-cross morphemes must be a word or a sentence, it is obviously impossible—in the final symbolic transcription of an English sentence—to have a bound morpheme isolated in such a fashion. That is (again, in the final symbolic transcription), there is no symbol: $*#Z_1#$. And it is exactly this fact, namely, that a bound morpheme cannot be permitted to remain isolated between a pair of word boundary symbols, that accounts for every occurrence of *to do* as an auxiliary in English. We shall examine this in more detail in Chapter 7.

The following transformation applies to a terminal string of the phrase-structure derivation:

T 5.6 $X + Y \Longrightarrow X \# Y$

where X is any terminal symbol and Y is any terminal symbol except a suffix (e.g., Af, $\emptyset_2$, Z_2).

Rule T 5.6 says we are to insert a word boundary symbol between every two symbols in a terminal string except in two special cases. We must not insert such a symbol between any noun and the following affix, or between any verb (i.e., any *Modal, have, be, V_i, V_t, V_c,* and so on) and a following affix. Take as an example the derivation given in Chapter 3 for Sentence 3.9: *The child could see the monsters.* After applying the affix (flip-flop) transformation, we have the following string:

> *the + child + $\emptyset_2$ + can + Pas + see + the + monster + Z_2*

According to the new rule of sentence boundary, this string

should be preceded and followed by a double cross:

$$\#the + child + \emptyset_2 + can + Pas + see + the + monster + Z_2\#$$

Now, applying T 5.6 we can insert word boundaries between all the symbols except in the cases noted:

$$\#the \# child + \emptyset_2 \# can + Pas \# see \# the \# monster + Z_2\#$$

We have now isolated all the words in the sentence. The morphographemic rules will give the final shape for such things as $child + \emptyset_2$ and $can + Pas$.[9]

We can now remove the restriction on the affix (flip-flop) transformation by rewriting the transformation so it includes a word boundary. That is, we want to have the transformation in the following form:

T 5.2 $\quad Af + v \Longrightarrow v + Af\#$

This transformation must be applied *before* the word boundary transformation (otherwise the Af will become attached to the wrong v). If the proper order is followed — first, flip-flop, then word boundary — every affix will automatically be attached to the proper stem.

We can illustrate these operations by taking a sentence with a long auxiliary phrase: *The boy may have been sleeping.* This sentence has the following derivation:

$\quad\quad \# S \#$
1. $Nom + VP$
2. $Nom + Aux + MV$
3. $Nom + Tn + Modal + have + en + be + ing + MV$
4. $Nom + Tn + Modal + have + en + be + ing + V_i$

---

[9] In the experience of the author, some students overlook a distinction inherent in the rule when they first come to apply it. In particular, these students fail to see why we must place a word boundary symbol between *Pas* (which is clearly an affix) and *see* (which is clearly a verb). They are, in this case, reading the rule backwards. The rule does not make an exception for $Af + v$; rather, the exceptions are concerned only with the reverse order of these symbols, viz., $v + Af$. In short, we *must* place a word boundary between any two symbols that are not specifically a case of either $N + \emptyset_2$ (or Z_2) or $v + Af$.

5. $Det + N + N^{\underline{o}} + Tn + Modal + have + en + be + ing + V_i$
6. $Det + N + \emptyset_2 + Tn + Modal + have + en + be + ing + V_i$
7. $\#Det + N + \emptyset_2 + Pres + Modal + have + en + be + ing + V_i\#$

This is the terminal string of the phrase-structure derivation. We then apply the agreement transformation:

8. $\#Det + N + \emptyset_2 + Z_1 + Modal + have + en + be + ing + V_i\#$

Now we apply the new flip-flop transformation:

9. $\#Det + N + \emptyset_2 + Modal + Z_1 \# have + be + en \# V_i + ing \#$

(In theory, after flip-flopping $ing + V_i$ to get $V_i + ing\#$ we should have *two* double-cross symbols at the end: one which indicates the end of the sentence and another which is automatically inserted by the transformation. In practice, however, most linguists omit the duplicated symbol.)

And finally, we apply the word boundary transformation. Notice, however, that it is not necessary to insert a word boundary symbol between two morphemes if one is already present:

10. $\#Det \# N + \emptyset_2 \# Modal + Z_1 \# have \# be + en \# V_i + ing \#$

Inserting words from the lexicon and applying the relevant morphographemic rules will reduce this string to:

Sentence 5.59   The boy may have been sleeping.

The fourth model grammar which follows omits some of the material included in earlier models. To repeat an earlier observation, the model grammars given in this text are not intended to duplicate a scientific grammar of English. They are merely a pedagogical device for acquainting the reader with the theory that underlies transformational generative grammar.

This fourth model grammar is also the last given in the body of the text. We shall, of course, continue to discuss transformations and phrase-structure rules, but it will not always be necessary to characterize them formally. In addition, we will simplify many branching tree diagrams so that they emphasize the material under discussion. We shall, in short, ignore many of the detailed refinements of a scientific grammar of English and concentrate instead on those aspects of the theory that have particular relevance to the teacher of English.[10]

Our initial string is: # S #

A. Base Rules

Phrase Structure

PS 5.1 $S \longrightarrow Nom + VP$

PS 5.2 $VP \longrightarrow Aux + MV$

PS 5.3 $MV \longrightarrow \begin{Bmatrix} be + Pred \\ V \end{Bmatrix} (Adv)$

PS 5.4 $V \longrightarrow \begin{Bmatrix} V_i \\ V_t + Nom \\ V_c + Adj \end{Bmatrix}$

PS 5.5 $Aux \longrightarrow Tn \ (Modal) \ (have + en) \ (be + ing)$

PS 5.6 $Pred \longrightarrow \begin{Bmatrix} Nom \\ Adj \\ Loc \end{Bmatrix}$

PS 5.7 $Nom \longrightarrow Det + N + N^{\underline{o}} \ (+S)$

PS 5.8 $N^{\underline{o}} \longrightarrow \begin{Bmatrix} \emptyset_2 \\ Z_2 \end{Bmatrix}$

---

[10] Readers of a more scientific bent can consult the Bibliography for a list of articles and books that contain a wide variety of phrase-structure and transformational rules.

PS 5.9 $Det \longrightarrow \begin{Bmatrix} Art \\ Dem \\ wh\text{-} \end{Bmatrix}$

PS 5.10 $Tn \longrightarrow \begin{Bmatrix} Pres \\ \\ Pas \end{Bmatrix}$

Lexicon

N: child, man, monster, pterodactyl

Art: a, every (singular only); all, both (plural only); the, some (singular or plural)

V_i: sleep, dance

V_c: look

Adj: lonesome, happy

Adv: today

Dem: this, that (singular only); these, those (plural only)

V_t: see, entertain

Modal: may, will

Loc: here, there

B.   Transformations

T 5.1 $\begin{bmatrix} NP_s \\ NP_p \end{bmatrix} + Pres \Longrightarrow \begin{bmatrix} NP_s + Z_1 \\ NP_p + \emptyset_1 \end{bmatrix}$

T 5.2 $Af + v \Longrightarrow v + Af \# \ (Af = \emptyset_1, Z_1, Pas, \text{-}en, \text{-}ing)$

T 5.3 $\begin{bmatrix} NP_s \\ NP_p \end{bmatrix} + be + Pas \Longrightarrow \begin{bmatrix} NP_s + was \\ NP_p + were \end{bmatrix}$

T 5.4 $Det + N_{matrix} + N^{\underline{o}} \ (+ \ Det + N_{const} + N^{\underline{o}} + be + Adj)$
   $\Longrightarrow Det + Adj + N_{matrix} + N^{\underline{o}}$
   where $N_{matrix} + N^{\underline{o}} = N_{const} + N^{\underline{o}}$

T 5.5 $wh\text{-} + \begin{bmatrix} N_{an} \\ N_{in} \end{bmatrix} \Longrightarrow \begin{bmatrix} who \\ which, that \end{bmatrix}$

т 5.6 $X + Y \Longrightarrow X \# Y$

where X is any terminal symbol, and Y is any terminal symbol except a suffix.

C. Morphographemic Rules

As before we shall assume that the morphographemic rules are obvious. We may, however, add one final rule: "Remove all boundary symbols, capitalize the first letter of the string, and place a period after the last word."

Like the third model grammar, this model will produce an infinite number of sentences. The artificial limitations of the lexicon, however, would make the sentences rather boring. For illustrative purposes, we shall generate two sentences: Sentence 5.60 *Both monsters will entertain the child today* (a kernel sentence which contains no embedded elements), and Sentence 5.61 *The pterodactyl may have seen the man who was sleeping* (a derived sentence which consists of a kernel matrix—*The pterodactyl may have seen the man*—and an embedded constituent—*The man was sleeping*).

Sentence 5.60   Both monsters will entertain the child today.

$\# S \#$

1. $Nom + VP$	(PS 5.1)
2. $Nom + Aux + MV$	(PS 5.2)
3. $Nom + Aux + V + Adv$	(PS 5.3)
4. $Nom + Aux + V_t + Nom + Adv$	(PS 5.4)
5. $Nom + Tn + Modal + V_t + Nom + Adv$	(PS 5.5)
6. $Det + N + N^{\underline{o}} + Tn + Modal + V_t + Det + N + N^{\underline{o}}$ $+ Adv$	(PS 5.7)
7. $Det + N + Z_2 + Tn + Modal + V_t + Det + N + \emptyset_2$ $+ Adv$	(PS 5.8)
8. $Art + N + Z_2 + Tn + Modal + V_t + Art + N + \emptyset_2$ $+ Adv$	(PS 5.9)
9. $\#Art + N + Z_2 + Pres + Modal + V_t + Art + N$ $+ \emptyset_2 + Adv\#$	(PS 5.10)

Line No. 9 is the terminal string of the phrase-structure derivation. We now insert words from the lexicon:

10. *#both + monster + Z_2 + Pres + will + entertain + the + child + $\emptyset_2$ + today#*

And then we apply the relevant transformations:

11. *#both + monster + Z_2 + $\emptyset_1$ + will + entertain + the + child + $\emptyset_2$ + today#*   (T 5.1)
12. *#both + monster + Z_2 + will + $\emptyset_1$ # entertain + the + child + $\emptyset_2$ + today#*   (T 5.2)
13. *#both # monster + Z_2 # will + $\emptyset_1$ # entertain # the # child + $\emptyset_2$ # today#*   (T 5.6)

The relevant morphographemic rules, including the final one given in the fourth model grammar, will then change this string to:

Sentence 5.60   Both monsters will entertain the child today.

The second derivation is only slightly more complex:

Sentence 5.61   The pterodactyl may have seen the man who was sleeping.

 # S #
1. *Nom + VP*   (PS 5.1)
2. *Nom + Aux + MV*   (PS 5.2)
3. *Nom + Aux + V*   (PS 5.3)
4. *Nom + Aux + V_t + Nom*   (PS 5.4)
5. *Nom + Tn + Modal + have + en + V_t + Nom*   (PS 5.5)
6. *Det + N + $N^{\underline{o}}$ + Tn + Modal + have + en + V_t + Det + N + $N^{\underline{o}}$ (+S)*   (PS 5.7)
7. *Det + N + $\emptyset_2$ + Tn + Modal + have + en + V_t + Det + N + $\emptyset_2$ (+S)*   (PS 5.8)
8. *Art + N + $\emptyset_2$ + Tn + Modal + have + en + V_t + Art + N + $\emptyset_2$ (+S)*   (PS 5.9)
9. *#Art + N + $\emptyset_2$ + Pres + Modal + have + en + V_t + Art + N + $\emptyset_2$ (+S)#*   (PS 5.10)

Line No. 9 is the terminal string of the matrix sentence.

1a. $Nom + VP$ (PS 5.1)
2a. $Nom + Aux + MV$ (PS 5.2)
3a. $Nom + Aux + V$ (PS 5.3)
4a. $Nom + Aux + V_i$ (PS 5.4)
5a. $Nom + Tn + be + ing + V_i$ (PS 5.5)
6a. $Det + N + N^{\underline{o}} + Tn + be + ing + V_i$ (PS 5.7)
7a. $Det + N + \emptyset_2 + Tn + be + ing + V_i$ (PS 5.8)
8a. $wh\text{-} + N + \emptyset_2 + Tn + be + ing + V_i$ (PS 5.9)
9a. $wh\text{-} + N + \emptyset_2 + Pas + be + ing + V_i$ (PS 5.10)

Line No. 9a is the terminal string of the constituent sentence (notice that no sentence boundaries are indicated). We now embed the terminal string of the constituent sentence into the matrix sentence:

10. $\#Art + N + \emptyset_2 + Pres + Modal + have + en + V_t$ $+ Art + N + \emptyset_2 + wh\text{-} + N + \emptyset_2 + Pas + be + ing$ $+ V_i\#$

And add words from the lexicon:

11. $\#the + pterodactyl + \emptyset_2 + Pres + may + have$ $+ en + see + the + man + \emptyset_2 + wh\text{-} + man + \emptyset_2 + Pas$ $+ be + ing + sleep\#$

And then apply the relevant transformations:

12. $\#the + pterodactyl + \emptyset_2 + Z_1 + may + have + en$ $+ see + the + man + \emptyset_2 + wh\text{-} + man + \emptyset_2 + Pas$ $+ be + ing + sleep\#$ (T 5.1)
13. $\#the + pterodactyl + \emptyset_2 + may + Z_1 \# have + see$ $+ en \# the + man + \emptyset_2 + wh\text{-} + man + \emptyset_2 + be + Pas$ $\# sleep + ing\#$ (T 5.2)
14. $\#the + pterodactyl + \emptyset_2 + may + Z_1 \# have + see$ $+ en \# the + man + \emptyset_2 + wh\text{-} + man + \emptyset_2 + was$ $\# sleep + ing\#$ (T 5.3)
15. $\#the + pterodactyl + \emptyset_2 + may + Z_1 \# have + see$ $+ en \# the + man + \emptyset_2 + who + was \# sleep + ing\#$ (T 5.5)

16. *#the # pterodactyl + ∅₂ # may + Z₁ # have*
    # see + en # the # man + ∅₂ # who # was # sleep
    + ing#   (T 5.6)

And finally apply the relevant morphographemic rules:

Sentence 5.61   The pterodactyl may have seen the man who
was sleeping.

The branching tree diagrams for the surface structure and
the deep structure of this nonkernel sentence are given
on pages 146–47.

5.5 SUMMARY

The emphasis throughout this chapter has been on the
English verb system. In particular, we have noted that
main verbs can be divided into four major classes: (1) *to be*,
(2) intransitive, (3) transitive, and (4) copulative. The last
three classes all have several varieties of subclasses. Some
transitive verbs, for example, cannot form a passive. Others
must be followed by animate objects. And still others can
be followed by direct objects and objective complements.

We then examined the auxiliary verbs and found that
they can be represented with a simple phrase-structure
rule. And we also found that the entire system of verb
forms in the indicative mood, active voice, can be represented by a single formula:

$Tn\ (Modal)\ (have + en)\ (be + ing)\ MV$

This formula, in conjunction with the flip-flop transformation, will generate all the tenses of the active voice, indicative mood.

Finally, we presented the last model grammar, and, in
particular, we illustrated the recursive property of the
grammar again by embedding a constituent sentence into
a matrix to produce what is traditionally known as a complex sentence. We are now ready to look at various other
kinds of modification.

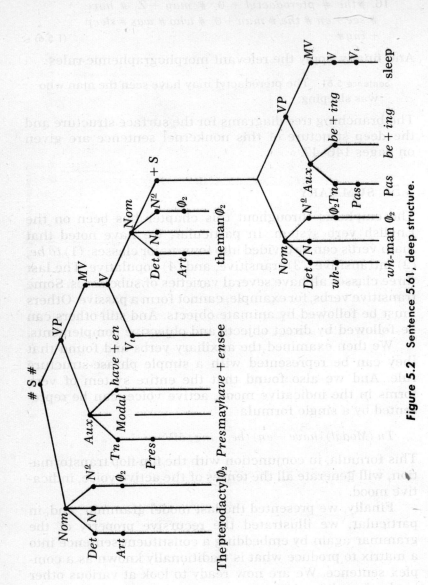

Figure 5.2 Sentence 5.61, deep structure.

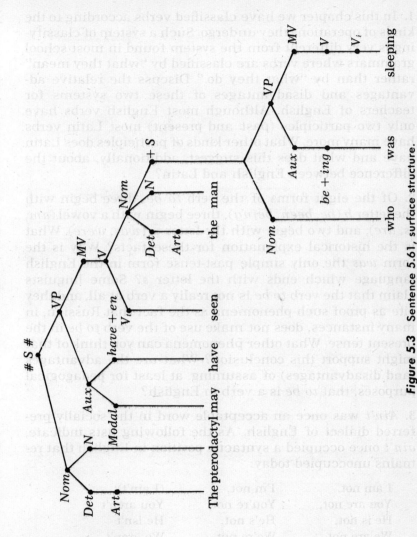

Figure 5.3 Sentence 5.61, surface structure.

147

Discussion

1. In this chapter we have classified verbs according to the kinds of operations they undergo. Such a system of classifying is very different from the system found in most school grammars where verbs are classified by "what they mean" rather than by "what they do." Discuss the relative advantages and disadvantages of these two systems for teachers of English. Although most English verbs have only two participles (past and present) most Latin verbs have many more. What other kinds of participles does Latin have and what does this suggest, additionally, about the difference between English and Latin?

2. Of the eight forms of the verb *to be*, three begin with the letter *b* (*be, been, being*), three begin with a vowel (*am, is, are*), and two begin with the letter *w* (*was, were*). What is the historical explanation for these facts? Why is the form *was* the only simple past-tense form in the English language which ends with the letter *s*? Some linguists claim that the verb *to be* is not really a verb at all, and they cite as proof such phenomena as the fact that Russian, in many instances, does not make use of the verb *to be* in the present tense. What other phenomena can you think of that might support this conclusion? What are the advantages (and disadvantages) of assuming, at least for pedagogical purposes, that *to be* is a verb in English?

3. *Ain't* was once an acceptable word in the socially preferred dialect of English. As the following lists indicate, *ain't* once occupied a syntactic position in English that remains unoccupied today:

I am not,	I'm not,	(I ain't)
You are not,	You're not,	You aren't
He is not,	He's not,	He isn't
We are not,	We're not,	We aren't
They are not,	They're not,	They aren't

How and why did *ain't* become unacceptable in the socially preferred dialect? What does this imply about the systematic character of language? What forces operate on language to change it? How do you, in your dialect, complete the third tag question given below:

1. They are going, aren't they?
2. He is going, isn't he?
3. I am going, _____?

Compare your answer with those of several other people from different parts of the country.

4. The text notes that we use many verbs as if they were modals. In addition to *need* and *dare* we frequently use such constructions as *ought to* and *be going to* (e.g., *I ought to have gone; I ought to be going; I'm going to be calling on him in a few days*). Check some literal transcription of speech (such as the record of a trial) and see what other "near-modals" you can find.

5. We have not considered the various means of creating new verbs in English. (In contrast, we did consider new methods of creating nouns.) How do we create new verbs? How do these means of creating verbs compare with the nominalizations that were discussed in Chapter 4? What do these facts suggest about the validity of the statement found in many school grammars: "the verb is the most important word in the sentence."

Exercises

1. Construct derivations and branching tree diagrams for the following sentences:

1. Those children have been sleeping.
2. Every man who dances here will be happy today.

2. Rewrite phrase-structure rule PS 5.9 so that it is capable of generating the italicized phrases in the following sentences:

1. *A group of* children saw the monsters.
2. The man saw *a brace of* pterodactyls.
3. *This group of* men entertained *that brace of* pterodactyls.

3. Construct a transformation that will produce the italicized nominals in the following sentences:

1. I like *dancing.* I like *to dance.*
2. I like *entertaining.* I like *to entertain.*

4. Construct a branching tree diagram for Sentence 5.60.

⟨6⟩

Adjectives and Adverbs

Modified rapture!

w. s. GILBERT, *The Mikado*

To quote W. S. Gilbert out of context, we might say that adjectives and adverbs bring "modified rapture" to the heart of a grammarian. The notion of modification is certainly important in English, and it merits our undivided, if not rapt, attention.

The traditional school-grammar definitions of adjective and adverb both hinge on the word "modify":

An adjective is a word used to modify a noun.
An adverb is a word used to modify a verb, adjective, or
  other adverb.

If we could develop some syntactic way of defining the word "modify," then perhaps we could utilize these definitions, with a few minor changes, in a transformational grammar of English.

Sometimes grammarians say that a modifier is a word used **attributively**. Semantically, this means that an adjective, for example, symbolizes some attribute or quality possessed by the person or thing that a particular noun symbolizes. The full implications of this notion are difficult to discuss, since philosophers and logicians have yet to determine "how a word means." Syntactically, however, and as a first step toward understanding the semantic implications, we can define at least some sense of "attribute" and this can form a basis for a related definition of "modify." For our purposes then, and in accordance with the intuitive feelings of native speakers and philosophers alike, we can say that sentences having the following form are a syntactic definition of the notion "attribute":

$$Nom + be + Adj_d$$

In other words, the **descriptive adjective** (Adj_d) in sentences of this type is, by definition, attributive to the *Nom*.

More formally, and paraphrasing Lees, we may now say that an adjective "is any word which is an expansion of the English grammatical category *Adj* in an English grammar, or a transformational replacement of such a word."[1] With these two definitions as a basis, we can turn to a more detailed investigation of adjectives and adverbs. In particular, we can considerably enlarge the discussion of these two categories presented in an earlier chapter.

6.1 ADJECTIVES

The previous discussion of adjectives, in Chapter 4, omitted many significant facts. With very little elaboration, the discussion simply grouped together, as adjectives, all lexical words that could replace the symbol *Adj* in sentences having the form *Nom* + *be* + *Adj*. We also noticed that such words could generally be embedded from a constituent sentence into a matrix sentence. But we did not make any other distinctions.

In particular, we did not distinguish between **regular** and **derived adjectives**, or between those that describe inherent attributes and those that describe accidental attributes. We said nothing about degrees of adjectives, or about restrictions on prenominal and postnominal occurrence. Yet these things are all important in English.

---

[1] Lees, *Report on the Eleventh Annual Round Table Meeting on Linguistics and Language Studies*, p. 1.

Transformational linguists have been investigating adjectives for several years. A large percentage of their time has been spent on comparative constructions, but much of this work is probably due for re-evaluation in light of the most recent advances in the general theory of transformational grammar. On the other hand, there are certain facts that appear to be well defined and that account successfully for a native speaker's intuition about the system of adjectives in English. We can begin an investigation of these facts by noting the distinction between regular (or **base**) adjectives and those that are derived by transformations from other parts of speech.

Base and Derived Adjectives. Base adjectives contain no derivational suffixes; that is, they have not been made into adjectives from some other grammatical category. The majority of base adjectives are words of one syllable:

tall, young, hot, sad, green, good, bright, large

Many, however, have two syllables:

common, happy, pretty, quiet, ugly

Derived adjectives are constructed from other parts of speech by the addition, transformationally, of one of the many allomorphs of the various adjectivalization transformations. The vast majority of derived adjectives were originally nouns or verbs. They can be classified according to the various operations that transform them into adjectives. Thus the large group of intransitive verbs that do not require a following adverb of location generally have present participles that can function as adjectives:

Sentence 6.1 *The baby may have slept.* ⟹ *The sleeping baby* . . .

Sentence 6.2 *The secretary was dancing.* ⟹ *The dancing secretary* . . .

Sentence 6.3 *The instructor has fainted.* ⟹ *The fainting instructor* . . .

The past participles of most verbs that relate to cooking can be used as adjectives that describe food which is ready to serve:[2]

Sentence 6.4   *She may bake some beans.* ⟹ *The baked beans* ...

Sentence 6.5   *She is frying chicken.* ⟹ *The fried chicken* ...

We may even have:

Sentence 6.6   *She burned the toast.* ⟹ *The burnt toast* ...

Both the present and the past participles of verbs that require animate objects can be used as adjectives:

The terrified boy ...
Her pleasing smile ...
His astonished glance ...
Their surprised parents ...

Obviously, these are only a few of the many classes of verbs that can be transformed into single-word adjectives. But the regularity of these examples suggests that linguists, as they develop the scientific grammar of English more completely, will probably be able to formulate many generalized rules for constructing adjectives from verbs.

Nouns also show a wide variety in the forms they take when transformed into single-word adjectives:

childish, faulty, hopeful, fatal, marvelous, roofed

As with the verbs, there are subclasses of nouns that behave alike under adjectivalization:

hopeful	marvelous	childish
truthful	wondrous	boyish
faithful	joyous	girlish

But the rules for transforming nouns into single-word ad-

---

[2] Actually, the past participles of all verbs that take concrete objects (and no other complements) behave exactly like verbs of cooking.

jectives will be more complex, or at least more numerous, than the similar rules for verbs because of the greater number of adjectivalization suffixes that can be attached to nouns:

joyful	childish	manly
wonderful	boyish	childlike

But the following cannot be formed:

*marvelful

Embedding Adjectives. Having established a distinction between base and derived adjectives, we can now turn to some fundamental operational distinctions. We have already seen how a constituent sentence can be embedded behind any noun in a matrix sentence. As both Lees and Carlota S. Smith have pointed out, the most natural system of introducing adjectives into a matrix sentence has three sequential parts.

First, a constituent sentence is introduced into a matrix sentence as a postnominal relative clause. For example, if we are given the matrix

Sentence 6.7a   John is the man

and the constituent

Sentence 6.7b   The man is most likely to succeed

we can get

Sentence 6.7c   John is the man who is most likely to succeed.

Second, when the verb in the constituent is some form of *to be*, we can frequently delete the verb and the preceding *wh-* word:

Sentence 6.7d   John is the man most likely to succeed.

And third, we can generally—but not always—move the adjective into a prenominal position.

Sentence 6.7e   John is the most likely man to succeed.

There are, however, certain restrictions on introducing adjectives into a matrix sentence.

The first rule, in which a constituent sentence is introduced into a matrix as a relative clause, establishes a basis for most of the restrictions on adjectives. Consider the following sentences:[3]

Sentence 6.8 Marge, who paints well, makes her own cards.
Sentence 6.9 Any man who likes George Eliot is a connoisseur.

The following are not acceptable:

*Marge who cooks well likes smoked salmon.
*Any man, who likes Dickens, is gregarious.

These examples indicate the two types of relative clauses, generally called **restrictive** and **nonrestrictive**. In this text, we shall adopt the distinction common among transformational grammarians of restrictive and **appositive**. Restrictive clauses are not separated by punctuation from the nouns they modify; appositive clauses, like an analogous noun in apposition, are separated by an intervening comma.

Some noun phrases can be followed by either restrictive or appositive clauses, some only by restrictive clauses, and some only by appositive clauses. The determining factor is the degree of definiteness of the determiner-plus-noun combination.

Carlota Smith suggests three levels of definiteness, using the following descriptive terms: **unique** (i.e., in which the determiner is $\emptyset$ — zero — as in the case of proper names), **specified**, and **unspecified**. She notes that nouns with unspecified determiners, such as *any* and *all*, can only be followed by restrictive clauses; nouns with specified determiners, such as *the*, can be followed by both restrictive and appositive clauses; and unique nouns can be followed by appositive clauses only.

---

[3] This general discussion is based largely on the work of Carlota S. Smith. Some of her operations, however, have been revised in accordance with recent advances in transformational theory.

This analysis explains why we can say:

Sentence 6.10a   My sister Jeanne ⎫
Sentence 6.10b   My sister, Jeanne, ⎬ is a good horsewoman.
Sentence 6.10c   Jeanne, my sister, ⎭

But we cannot say:

*Jeanne my sister is a good horsewoman.

The levels of definiteness also affect the second rule, i.e., the rule pertaining to the ability to delete *wh-* and *to be*. For example, we can say:

Sentence 6.11a   Ann, who was tired of reading Johnson, was also tired of life.
Sentence 6.11b   Ann, tired of reading Johnson, was also tired of life.

But we cannot say:

*Mike who was tired of Johnson was also tired of life.
*Mike tired of Johnson and was also tired of life.

Similarly, the degree of definiteness in the determiner-plus-noun combination also affects the operation of the transformation that embeds adjectives in a prenominal position. With one exception, nearly all single-word adjectives can—and, in general, must—be embedded before a noun when we delete the subject and the verb of the relative clause (i.e., the *wh-* and *to be*):

Sentence 4.9c   God who is invisible created the world which is visible.
Sentence 4.9d   Invisible God created the visible world.
Sentence 6.12a   He bought a car which is green.
Sentence 6.12b   He bought a green car.

But this transformation does not take place if the noun in the matrix sentence is closely related to a PRO form, that is, if it is a personal pronoun or an indefinite word such as *someone* or *something*. Pronouns can only be modified by appositive clauses; single-word adjectives generally follow words like *someone* and *something*:

Sentence 6.13 Something good will happen to those who know grammar.

Sentence 6.14 She wants to marry someone tall.

Classes of Adjectives. Certain adjectives also behave differently from certain other adjectives with respect to three kinds of transformations. In the first case, we are concerned with those adjectives which can be *followed* by factive nominals. Consider the following sentences, all of which contain factive nominals:

Sentence 6.15 The boy is happy that she works.

Sentence 6.16 I feel certain that she can drive.

Sentence 6.17 The girl seemed sorry that she bought the dress.

But the following are not acceptable:

*The boy is clever that she works.
*I am good that she can drive.

Following Lees, we can call the adjectives which can be *followed* by factive nominals Adj_x. The category includes such adjectives as: *afraid, ashamed, aware, certain, glad, happy, proud, sorry, sure*. The matrix sentence might have the following shape (V_{ap} includes the copulative verbs of appearance *seem, appear*):

$$Nom_{an} + \begin{Bmatrix} V_{ap} \\ be \end{Bmatrix} + Adj_x + \begin{Bmatrix} of \\ about \end{Bmatrix} + SOMETHING \ (+S)$$

The constituent sentence, which can be of any form, is nominalized by placing a *that* in front of it (that is, it is transformed into a factive nominal as we have seen in Chapter 4) and is then substituted from the PRO form: The preposition is deleted at the same time. Thus we have:

Sentence 6.18a The boy is happy about *SOMETHING*.

Sentence 6.18b She works.

Sentence 6.18c   The boy is happy about *SOMETHING* (that she works).

Sentence 6.18d   The boy is happy that she works.

The second class of adjectives, which Lees designates as Adj_y, can be followed by infinitival nominals rather than by factive nominals. Consider the following sentences, all of which contain infinitival nominals:

Sentence 6.19   The boy seems determined to leave.

Sentence 6.20   The girl is eager to please.

Sentence 6.21   The man appears certain to buy the car.

The following is not acceptable:

*The woman is aware to stay.

As the examples suggest, many of the Adj_x class of adjectives can also function in the Adj_y class. In general, this latter class includes such words as: *determined, loath, prepared, prone, ready, anxious, apt, content, glad, eager.* Adjectives that undergo this transformation occur in matrix sentences having the form:

$$Nom + \begin{Bmatrix} V_{ap} \\ be \end{Bmatrix} + Adj_y + Prep + SOMETHING\ (+S)$$

where the particular preposition is determined by the adjective meaning: "determined about *SOMETHING*," "prepared for *SOMETHING*," "glad of *SOMETHING*," "eager for *SOMETHING*." Consider these examples:

Sentence 6.22a   The boy seems determined about *SOMETHING.*

Sentence 6.22b   The boy leaves.

Sentence 6.22c   The boy seems determined about *SOMETHING* (the boy to leave).

Sentence 6.22d   The boy seems determined to leave.

In this case, both the preposition and the repeated nominal are deleted by the transformation.

The third class of adjectives, Adj_z, includes words such as: *clever, good, silly, smart, wise.* These adjectives can be preceded by factive nominals or *followed* by transformationally related infinitival nominals. Again there is some overlap between this class and the other classes. But notice:

> Sentence 6.23a   John is fortunate to love Mary.
> Sentence 6.23b   That John loves Mary is fortunate.
> Sentence 6.24a   The boy is smart to go.
> Sentence 6.24b   That the boy goes is smart.[4]

Contrast these occurrences of Adj_z with an occurrence of an Adj_y:

> Sentence 6.25   The boy is anxious to leave.

But the following is not acceptable:

> *That the boy leaves is anxious.

> Sentence 6.26   The girl is eager to please.

The following is not acceptable:

> *That the girl pleases is eager.

In other words, the fact that both Adj_y and Adj_z can be followed by infinitives is an accidental surface characteristic that conceals a deep difference between them.

We can sum up these remarks on Adj_x, Adj_y, and Adj_z as follows:

A. The Adj_x class of adjectives, which can be followed by such prepositions as *of* and *for* (as well as by a PRO form), can also be followed by factive nominals that substitute for the preposition and the PRO form. Thus we have:

> Sentence 6.27a   John is certain of *SOMETHING.*
> Sentence 6.27b   John is certain that Mary is going.

---

[4] This transformation is not possible in all dialects of American English.

B. The Adj_y class of adjectives, which can be followed by prepositions and a PRO form, can also be followed by infinitival nominals that substitute for the preposition and the PRO form. Thus we have:

Sentence 6.28a   Mary is eager for SOMETHING.
Sentence 6.28b   Mary is eager to buy a new hat.

C. The Adj_z class of adjectives bears some resemblance to the Adj_y class, since they can also be followed by an infinitive. But in addition, the infinitive that follows any Adj_z is related transformationally to a factive nominal that can occupy position one in a similar sentence. For example:

Sentence 6.29a   That John types all his term papers is wise.
Sentence 6.29b   John is wise to type all his term papers.

Before leaving the topic of adjectives, we should note a distinction first recognized by Lees.[5] Adjectives that describe inherent properties cannot be followed by locative adverbs. Consequently, they contrast with adjectives that describe so-called accidental properties. Consider:

Sentence 6.30a   George is happy in New York.
Sentence 6.30b   George is happy.
Sentence 6.30c   George is intelligent.

The following, however, is not acceptable:

*George is intelligent in New York.

This distinction, coupled with the other distinctions we have already noted in connection with the kinds of constructions that can follow particular kinds of adjectives, suggests that in a complete scientific grammar adjectives will probably also be marked with a matrix convention similar to that adopted for nouns. When the symbol *Adj* occurs in a particular derivation, we will want to add certain restrictions on the kind of adjective that can be substituted for the symbol.

---

[5] Lees, *Grammar of English Nominalizations*, p. 12.

6.2 ADVERBS

After this lengthy digression away from the notion of modification we can turn to adverbs. But whereas adjectives can be called modifiers because they are transformationally related to a sentence having the form *Nom + be + Pred* (where *Pred* is *Adj$_a$*), we can immediately observe that not all words traditionally called adverbs can be grouped together under a similar definition.

To construct a similar definition that pertains to some adverbs, we need to recall the earlier statements about attribution. We also need to classify adverbs into several subcategories. In particular, we can identify five major subcategories of adverbs in English: (1) **sentence adverbials**, (2) **preverbs**, (3) **adverbs of location and time**, (4) **adverbs of manner**, and (5) **adverbs like "very," "quite," and "extremely"** which can precede adjectives and certain kinds of adverbs. We shall take up each of these in turn.

Sentence Adverbials. Sentence adverbials, as their name suggests, bear a syntactic relationship to the entire sentence rather than to some part. We have ignored them in the model grammars, but we can account for them with the first phrase-structure rule and with some transformations that are already available. Rule PS 6.1, as we have formulated it, is:

PS 6.1 $S \longrightarrow Nom + VP$

Suppose the matrix sentence resembles one of the following:

Sentence 6.31b   *SOMETHING* is certain.
Sentence 6.32b   *SOMETHING* is sure.

And suppose that the constituent sentence is one of the following (in this case, the constituent can have any form):

Sentence 6.31a   The semester is nearly over.
Sentence 6.32a   Hector bought three jugs.

If we now transform the constituent sentences into factive nominals and substitute them for the PRO forms in the relevant matrix sentences, we will have:

Sentence 6.31c That the semester is nearly over is certain.
Sentence 6.32c That Hector bought three jugs is sure.

These sentences obviously bear a transformational relationship to:

Sentence 6.31d Certainly the semester is nearly over.
Sentence 6.32d Surely Hector bought three jugs.

Since the adjective in the matrix is attributive to the factive nominal, and since the factive nominal is actually a transformation of a sentence, then we can easily see why the adverb derived from an adjective by a transformation of this kind is said to be attributive to the entire sentence. The constraints on which adjectives can be transformed by this process into sentence adverbials are identical with those on the occurrence of factive nominals following adjectives; that is, they are identical to those we have already examined in Chapter 4. In other words, sentence adverbials are attributive to entire sentences in exactly the same way that adjectives following the verb *to be* are attributive to subject nominals.[6]

Preverbs. In the opinion of the author the preverbs, as a group, are the least understood subclass of adverbs. Transformationalists generally include in this category such adverbs as *almost, always, ever* and *seldom, rarely, hardly.* They normally occur after the first auxiliary verb:

Sentence 6.33 John has almost finished the assignment.
Sentence 6.34 Mary is always eating.

---

[6] At present, linguists have not yet decided on the precise form of this transformation. The formulation given here will not, in fact, account for all sentence adverbials, e.g., *generally* and *particularly.* There is little doubt, however, that such words are ultimately related transformationally to an occurrence of *Nom + be + Pred*, where *Nom* is probably restricted to abstract nominals.

Sentence 6.35 Harry has seldom read a book.

Sentence 6.36 Guinevere has rarely arrived on time.

There are some restrictions on these forms. We cannot say:

*Guinevere has rarely arrived.

Negative preverbs (e.g., *seldom*) generally cannot co-occur with the negative morpheme {*Ng*} which, as we shall see in Chapter 7, is introduced as a "presentence" element and may be attached to an auxiliary verb. That is, there are no sentences of the form: **John hasn't seldom come.* This suggests a relationship between some preverbs and the negative morpheme which, however, has not yet been worked out by linguists.

Adverbs of Location and Time. Locative adverbs and adverbs of time, as we have already noticed, can occupy the fourth position in most sentences. Thus, we may have:

to be: Sentence 6.37 John is happy *in his new house.* (*Loc*)

Sentence 6.38 John is sad *today.* (*Tm*)

Type I: Sentence 6.39 Esther is swimming *in the river.* (*Loc*)

Sentence 6.40 The baby is sleeping *now.* (*Tm*)

Type II: Sentence 6.41 Quentin teaches school *in New York.* (*Loc*)

Sentence 6.42 Roger eats corn flakes *every day.* (*Tm*)

Type III: Sentence 6.43 Yorick seemed chopfallen *in his grave.* (*Loc*)

Sentence 6.44 Horatio grew sad *that day.* (*Tm*)

As these examples indicate, the occurrence of the preposition is sometimes optional, sometimes impossible, and sometimes obligatory. As an alternative to Sentence 6.44, we might say *on that day.* But we cannot, as an alternative to Sentence 6.38, say **on today.* Some of the rules governing the occurrence or nonoccurrence of the preposition can be explained on historical grounds; others are probably a factor of the relative frequency of the expression. If the rules can be made general enough, they can be included in the transformational part of the grammar; otherwise, the exceptions can be listed in the morphographemic rules.

In a pedagogical grammar of English, such as this one, adverbs of time and location are different from sentence adverbials and preverbs in a very significant way. As we have just seen, sentence adverbials can be derived from adjectives that have their origin in a constituent sentence; there is also some possibility that preverbs can be derived in a similar fashion. But in our analysis all adverbs of time are derived from a phrase-structure rule that expands *MV*. Consequently, they are not attributive as we have defined the term, since they are not transformationally related to *Pred*. Adverbs of location, however, can come from two sources: like adverbs of time, they can be introduced optionally in the phrase-structure rule which expands *MV*, or, like adjectives, they can be introduced from the symbol *Pred* in constituent sentences having the form *Nom + be + Pred* where *Pred* is rewritten, in this case, as *Loc*. Adverbs of location, then, can be called attributive if they can be traced back to the symbol *Pred*, but not if they are introduced in expanding the symbol *MV*. In the sentence *The house on the hill is old*, the adverbial prepositional phrase is attributive because it is derived from an embedded constituent sentence *The house is on the hill* (*Nom + be + Pred*). Conversely, in the sentence *They live on the hill*, the adverbial prepositional phrase is not attributive because it is derived from a *Loc* which was chosen optionally during the expansion of *MV* (*MV* $\longrightarrow$ *V + Adv*).

In contrast to sentence adverbials and preverbs, *Tm* and *Loc* are not based on adjectives but on adverbial PRO forms. More particularly, there are PRO forms underlying *Loc* and *Tm*:[7]

$$(at) \; SOMETIME, \quad \left(\left\{ \begin{matrix} at \\ \\ in \end{matrix} \right\} \right) SOME \; PLACE$$

---

[7] The parentheses around the braces $\left\{ \begin{matrix} in \\ at \end{matrix} \right\}$ indicate that the prepositions are optional.

We shall see the importance of these PRO forms when we discuss interrogatives in the following chapter. Now we need only notice that, parallel to the PRO forms for nouns, verbs, and determiners, there are PRO forms for adverbs of time and location. Thus, we may say:

Sentence 6.45a   I saw him *SOME PLACE* (PRO form)

Sentence 6.45b   I saw him there. (Single-word adverbial)

Sentence 6.45c   I saw him on the corner. (Adverbial prepositional phrase)

Adverbs of time are freely movable from their basic position to a new position immediately preceding the subject:

Sentence 6.46a   James saw a unicorn today.

Sentence 6.46b   Today James saw a unicorn.

Adverbs of location are slightly more restricted in their movement. This restriction is a consequence of the fact that any noun in English can be followed by an attributive adverb of location which is brought into position from a constituent sentence having the form $Nom + be + Loc$. Consider the following sentences:

Sentence 6.47   The children are drawing lions in the fourth grade.

Sentence 6.48   The children in the fourth grade are drawing lions.

Sentence 6.49   The children are drawing lions in their cages.

Sentence 6.50   The children in their cages are drawing lions.

In Sentence 6.47, the locative adverb is not attributive because it is an expansion of the symbol *Loc* which is optionally introduced in the phrase-structure rule that expands the symbol *MV*. In Sentences 6.48, 6.49, and 6.50, however, the locative adverb is attributive, since it is introduced from an optional constituent sentence following either the subject or direct object nominal. This can be easily shown in branching tree diagrams for the surface structure of Sentence 6.47 and Sentence 6.49 (see facing page). We can conjecture, then, that locative adverbs are

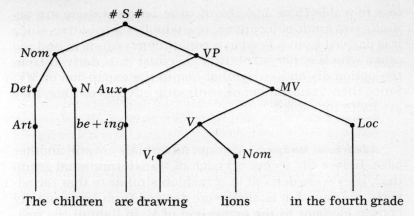

Figure 6.1   Sentence 6.47, surface structure.

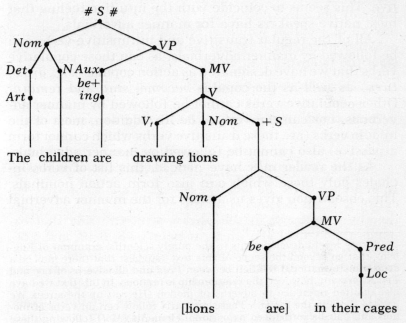

Figure 6.2   Sentence 6.49.

less movable than adverbs of time because there are actually two kinds of locatives: one which is attributive, since it is derived from a *Pred* in a constituent sentence; and the other which is not attributive, because it is derived from the optionally chosen symbol *Loc* in the expansion of *MV*. Since there is no danger of confusing adverbs of time, they are more movable.[8]

Adverbs of Manner. Manner adverbials are still another case. Before the recent revision of transformational grammar, they were derived in a fashion similar to that for adverbs of time; that is, they were derived from an optionally chosen element in the expansion of *V*. In light of the revision, it seems simplest to derive regular adverbs of manner from an embedded constituent sentence *Nom + be + Adj*, in which case, of course, they must be considered as attributive. This seems to coincide with the intuitive feeling that most native speakers have for manner adverbials.

All of the regular transitive and intransitive verbs can be followed by manner adverbials, as can those copulative verbs that we have designated as action copulas (e.g., *grow, turn*) as well as the copulas *become, stay* and *remain*. Other copulative verbs cannot be followed by manner adverbials, nor can the verb *to be*. In addition, most of the middle verbs (i.e., those transitive verbs which cannot form a passive) also cannot be followed by manner adverbials.

As the reader may have noticed, this list of verbs includes only those which can also form action nominals. This observation gives us a basis for the manner adverbial

---

[8] Very recent developments in the purely scientific grammar of English — that go beyond the scope of this text — suggest that there may be a deep transformational relation between *Pred* and all adverbs of *Loc* and *Tm*. At present, however, the relationship is tenuous. In this text we have also omitted reference to adverbs of motion (*He ran* up the street. *We walked* through the forest.). These regularly follow certain verbs of motion and can be introduced as optional elements (*Mot*) following these verbs.

transformation. Consider the following sentences:

Sentence 6.51a   The baby slept. (V_{in})

Sentence 6.51b   The baby's sleeping was peaceful. (*Nom +*
be + Adj)

Sentence 6.51c   The baby slept *peacefully*.

Sentence 6.52a   Jack Hawkins climbed the rigging. (V_t)

Sentence 6.52b   His climbing of the rigging was quick. (*Nom*
+ be + Adj)

Sentence 6.52c   Jack Hawkins climbed the rigging *quickly*.

Sentence 6.53a   Queen Victoria grew old. (V_{ac})

Sentence 6.53b   Her growing old was graceful. (*Nom + be*
+ Adj)

Sentence 6.53c   Queen Victoria grew old *gracefully*.

An asterisk precedes the sentences that are not acceptable
in the following group:

Vera is a teacher. (*to be*)
*Being of a teacher is superb. (*to be* cannot form an action
nominal)
*Vera is a teacher superbly.
I have five dollars. (V_{mid})
*Having of five dollars is careful. (*have* cannot form an
action nominal)
*I have five dollars carefully.

As these examples indicate, we need a matrix and a constituent sentence for this transformation. The matrix probably
has the form *SOMETHING + be + Adj*. But as is the case
with sentence adverbials, more work needs to be done on
the precise form of this transformation in a scientific grammar. It seems certain, however, that the adverb is ultimately derived from an Adj_d and is therefore attributive.

The manner adverbials we have been discussing are all
occurrences of $Adj_d + \{-ly\}$, where Adj_d stands for a descriptive adjective. We need to distinguish this class of adverbials from several other classes that are traditionally called
manner adverbials also. In particular, we need to make separate classes for concomitave and instrumental adverbials.

Consider:

Instrumental: *with my little finger, by force*, and so on.
Concomitave: *with his roommate, by himself*, and so on.

Thus we have:

Sentence 6.54   I will knock down the castle walls $\left\{\begin{array}{l}\text{with my fist.}\\ \text{by force.}\end{array}\right\}$

Sentence 6.55   My brother often studies $\left\{\begin{array}{l}\text{with his roommate.}\\ \text{by himself.}\end{array}\right\}$

These are obviously different from $Adj_d + \{-ly\}$. In particular, the instrumental is not attributive, since it is not derived from $Nom + be + Pred$; the concomitave adverb, however, is attributive (in Sentence 6.55, they are attributive to the subject).

Degree Adverbials.   Adverbs such as *very* and *quite* are most easily introduced into a phrase-structure derivation as optional elements preceding any descriptive adjective: $(Deg)\ Adj_d$. Thus they are an optional part of the descriptive adjective structure. We may have:

Sentence 6.56   Henry is young. $(Nom + be + Adj_d)$
Sentence 6.57   Henry is very young. $(Nom + be + Deg + Adj_d)$

In both these examples, *young* is attributive to *Henry*, and in Sentence 6.57, *very* indicates the degree of the adjective *young*.

Although there is also more work to be done on degree adverbials by transformational linguists, it seems to the author that they can best be derived from a PRO form: *to SOME DEGREE*. This PRO form would then lead to two sub-types: (1) single-word adverbials of degree (such as *very* and *quite*), and (2) prepositional phrases indicating degree (such as *to an extreme degree* and *to an obvious degree*). The adjectives in these prepositional phrases are all so-called **abstract adjectives**.

Thus, we might derive degree adverbials such as *extremely* as follows:

Sentence 6.58a   George is (Deg) tall.

Sentence 6.58b   George is (to *SOME DEGREE*) tall.
Sentence 6.58c   George is to some degree (+*S*) tall.
Sentence 6.58d   George is to a degree (which is extreme) tall.
Sentence 6.58e   George is to an extreme degree tall.

A transformation deletes the words *to an . . . degree* and replaces them with the adverbial morpheme {*-ly*}, to give:

Sentence 6.58f   George is extremely tall.

6.3   COMPARATIVE AND SUPERLATIVE DEGREES

These examples of degree adverbials refer only to the positive degree of the adjectives they modify. We obviously also want to introduce comparative and superlative degrees into the grammar. Again, the details have not been completely worked out by the transformational linguists, but to the author it seems probable that we can best introduce these various degrees in a phrase-structure rule that rewrites:

$$\text{PS 6.13} \quad Deg \longrightarrow \begin{Bmatrix} Pos \\ Comp + S \\ Super \end{Bmatrix}$$

Selecting *Pos* would give us the degree adverbials we have been discussing. We would then need another phrase-structure rule to expand *Comp*:

$$\text{PS 6.14} \quad Comp \longrightarrow \begin{Bmatrix} less \ldots than \\ as \ldots as \\ more \ldots than \end{Bmatrix}$$

Thus, to derive the sentence *Ron is as tall as John* we would go through the following steps:

Sentence 6.59a   Ron is (*Deg*) tall.
Sentence 6.59b   Ron is (*Comp + S*) tall.
Sentence 6.59c   Ron is (*as . . . as + S*) tall.
Sentence 6.59d   Ron is (*as . . . as + John is tall*) tall.

A transformation would then position the adjective of the

matrix (i.e., the *tall* of Sentence 6.59a) between the *as . . . as* and would delete the repeated words in the constituent (i.e., *is tall*), giving:

Sentence 6.59e   Ron is as tall as John.

Notice that this same series of steps (that is, the same phrase-structure and transformational rules) will also produce *Mary is less tall than Harry is wide*:

Sentence 6.60a   Mary is *(Deg)* tall.
Sentence 6.60b   Mary is *(Comp + S)* tall.
Sentence 6.60c   Mary is *(less . . . than + S)* tall.
Sentence 6.60d   Mary is *(less . . . than + Harry is wide)* tall.

As before, the transformation then places the adjective of the matrix (i.e., *tall*) between the discontinuous elements *less . . . than*. In this case, however, the *be + Pred* of the constituent sentence is not identical with the *be + Pred* of the matrix sentence and therefore cannot be deleted. Thus, we have:

Sentence 6.60e   Mary is less tall than Harry is wide.

Finally, the same series of steps will also produce sentences such as *Oliver is as tall as he is wide*:

Sentence 6.61a   Oliver is *(Deg)* tall.
Sentence 6.61b   Oliver is *(Comp + S)* tall.
Sentence 6.61c   Oliver is *(as . . . as + S)* tall.
Sentence 6.61d   Oliver is *(as . . . as + Oliver is wide)* tall.

In this case, the transformation places the adjective of the matrix (i.e., *tall*) between the discontinuous elements *as . . . as*. The *be + Pred* of the constituent is different from that of the matrix, and so it is not deleted. But the subject of the constituent is identical to the subject of the matrix and is therefore replaced by a pronoun, giving:

Sentence 6.61e   Oliver is as tall as he is wide.

To complete the discussion of comparatives, we need only note that in certain cases we may write *more + Adj* as *Adj* + {*er*}. There are, of course, certain restrictions on the form of the constituent sentence that must be built into any scientific grammar which need not concern us in a pedagogical grammar.

The symbol *Super* must also be rewritten to give the superlative degree of adjectives. Certainly the rewriting would introduce *the least* and *the most*. It will also introduce a discontinuous element, e.g., *the most . . . of* which would lead to phrases such as *Paris is* the most beautiful of *cities*.

6.4   SUMMARY

We can now return to the notion of modifier which was introduced early in the chapter. Any word in a sentence can be classified as a modifier (or, to use the term preferred by the author, an attributive; i.e., a word which symbolizes a particular attribute) if it is transformationally related to the symbol *Pred* in some sentence — either matrix or constituent — having the form *Nom* + *be* + *Pred*.

Thus nominals, adjectives, and locative adverbs may be attributive to other nominals as in the following examples:

Sentence 6.62   John, *my brother*, is a lawyer.
Sentence 6.63   The *tall* man ate the hotdog rapidly.
Sentence 6.64   The house *on the corner* was sold yesterday.

In addition, both restrictive and appositive clauses are also attributive (since they are derived from embedded sentences):

Sentence 6.65   The man *who bought the house* is very wealthy.
Sentence 6.66   The steak, *which was well done*, tasted good.

Sentence adverbials can be derived from adjectives that are attributive to factive nominals:

Sentence 6.67a   That John is happy is *certain*.
Sentence 6.67b   John is *certainly* happy.

In this pedagogical grammar preverbs and adverbs of time are not derived from *Pred*; thus, they cannot be called attributive. Adverbs of location can be called attributive only if they are derived from *Pred*; that is, they are not attributive if they are derived from the optionally chosen element *Loc* in the expansion of *MV*. Notice the following sentences:

Sentence 6.68   We never go there. (*never* is not attributive)

Sentence 6.69   We leave on Tuesday. (*on Tuesday* is not attributive)

Sentence 6.70   We work in New York. (*in New York* is not attributive)

Sentence 6.71   I saw the lion in his cage. (*in his cage* is attributive)

The locative in Sentence 6.71 is attributive because it is derived ultimately from a constituent sentence: *The lion is in his cage.*

Adverbs of manner are attributive only if they can be traced back to *Adj*$_d$ in a derivation. This requirement would include such manner adverbials as:

Sentence 6.72   The baby is sleeping *peacefully.*

Sentence 6.73   He grew old *gracefully.*

In short, transformational grammar provides a logical means of defining such terms as *modify* and *attributive,* and thus also provides an explanation for the traditional definitions of adjective and adverb.

Discussion

1. The definition of modification given in the text illustrates what a linguist means when he says that form (e.g., *Nom + be + Pred*) underlies meaning. In what ways are some of the other definitions in the text (e.g., those of subject, predicate, factive nominal, base adjective) also illustrative of this statement?

2. Consult the *Oxford English Dictionary* for the etymol-

ogies of the one- and two-syllable base adjectives given on p. 153. Compare these with the etymologies which the *OED* gives for the derived adjectives listed on p. 154. Can you think of any base adjectives that have been introduced into the language since the publication of the *OED*? any derived adjectives? What generalizations can you draw from these facts?

3. What are the advantages in referring to three levels of definiteness (i.e., unique, specified, and unspecified) rather than to two (i.e., definite and indefinite)? In what ways will an awareness of three levels rather than two assist in teaching proper punctuation? Is an awareness of the distinction more important for native speakers of English or for those studying English as a second language? Why?

4. What does the variety in the kinds of words traditionally called adverbs suggest about the school-grammar definition of adverb? What other flaws does the school-grammar definition have? How many different "parts of speech" can you list? What are the advantages and disadvantages of creating many part-of-speech categories (where every word in the category functions in exactly the same fashion as every other word) as opposed to creating a few categories (which are divided, as we have divided transitive verbs, into regular words — on the one hand — and those words which share some, but not all, of the features of the regular words — on the other hand)?

5. In the text, we have been careful to point out those places where transformational grammar is incomplete. In what ways are the traditional school grammars incomplete? Can the deficiencies of school grammars be corrected? Are school grammars self-consistent? Most school grammars define nouns and verbs semantically, that is, by what they mean; they define adjectives and adverbs (and most other parts of speech) syntactically, that is, by what they do (generally by what they do to nouns and verbs). What are some of the other inconsistencies? Can these inconsistencies be corrected?

Exercises

1. Select five consecutive pages from any modern novel and list all the adjectives that you find. What is the ratio of base adjectives to derived adjectives? How many different kinds of adjectivalization suffixes (i.e., allomorphs of the adjectivalization morpheme, such as *-ish* and *-ful*) can you find? Repeat this analysis with five consecutive pages taken from a Victorian or eighteenth-century novel or from a book on the history of art or the history of music.

2. Perform the same kind of analysis suggested in Exercise 1 for adverbs.

3. Construct a T rule for transforming descriptive adjectives into adverbs of manner. (Note: consider such sentences as *He ran around the track; the running was quick. The house burned to the ground; the burning was rapid.*)

4. Construct a simplified PS rule for rewriting *Super* (see p. 173), but ignoring the discontinuous elements, e.g., *the most . . . of.*

⟨7⟩

Rearranging the Basic Sentence

Prose = words in their best order.
COLERIDGE, *Table Talk.*

So far we have almost completely preserved the basic order of elements which was first presented in Chapter 2. That is, we have been content to concern ourselves with the four basic positions and with various methods of expanding these positions. We have not, however, investigated **interrogatives, passives,** or **imperatives,** all of which distort the basic sentence positions in some way. These are the primary subject of the present chapter.

7.1 INTERROGATIVES

Although all interrogatives are related, we can distinguish five primary subclasses that can be listed according to the kinds of words they question. That is, we can question nouns, verbs, adjectives, adverbs, and entire sentences.[1] Consider the following sentences:

Sentence 7.1   The small boy was sleeping under the tree.

Related to this sentence is a wide variety of questions:

Sentence 7.1a   Who was sleeping under the tree? (nominal question)

---

[1] The questioning of determiners (as in *How many boys were sleeping?*) is best treated with nominals since determiners are derived in the phrase-structure expansion of nominals (*Nom*).

Sentence 7.1b What was the small boy doing under the tree? (or) What did the small boy do under the tree? (verbal question, i.e., one which questions the verb)

Sentence 7.1c What kind of boy was sleeping under the tree? (adjectival question)

Sentence 7.1d Where was the boy sleeping? (adverbial question)

Sentence 7.1e Was the boy sleeping under the tree? (yes/no question, i.e., one which questions the entire sentence)

Sentence 7.1f The boy was sleeping under the tree, wasn't he? (tag question)

Sentence 7.1g The boy was sleeping under the tr$^{e^{e?}}$ (echo question)

In Chapter 3, we briefly mentioned the interrogative morpheme {Q}, but we gave no indication of how such a morpheme is introduced into the derivation of a sentence, nor did we discuss any interrogative transformations. We shall introduce {Q} as an optional element in the first phrase-structure rule:

PS 7.1 $S \longrightarrow (Q) Nom + VP$

Technically, {Q} is a **presentence element**. By way of preview, we may note here that there are several other presentence elements, including the negative morpheme {Ng}, the emphatic morpheme {Emph}, the imperative morpheme {Imp}, and (perhaps) the passive morpheme {by + Psv}. (In the scientific grammar of English, it may be more suitable to introduce the passive morpheme as an optional element following regular transitive verbs. In this text, we follow the latter option; that is, we assume the existence of an optional passive morpheme following every V_t.)

The presence of {Q} in the terminal string of a phrase-structure derivation will automatically trigger the interrogative transformation. This transformation, like many others, will actually be, in Chomsky's terms, a "family of transformations" that performs several operations. The particular operations that the transformation performs will be determined, in part, by the shape of the terminal string.

Any regular interrogative, however (that is, any interrogative except tag and echo questions), will invariably require one of the following operations:

$$\begin{bmatrix} Q + Nom + & Tn & + V \\ Q + Nom + Tn + Modal + X \\ Q + Nom + Tn + have & + X \\ Q + Nom + Tn + be & + X \end{bmatrix} \Longrightarrow$$

$$\begin{bmatrix} Tn & + Nom + V \\ Tn + Modal + Nom + X \\ Tn + have & + Nom + X \\ Tn + be & + Nom + X \end{bmatrix}$$

where $V = V_i, V_t, V_c$ and X may be anything.

If the question is to be a *wh-* interrogative, rather than a
simple yes/no question, we also need to perform another
operation. In particular, we need to move the element containing the *wh-* to the first position in the string.

Suppose we have the following strings:

Sentence 7.2a $Q + the\ boy + Tn + can + go$
Sentence 7.3a $Q + the\ boy + Tn + have + en + go$
Sentence 7.4a $Q + the\ boy + Tn + be + ing + go$

These strings correspond, respectively, to the strings in the
transformation represented by (1) $Tn + Modal$, (2) $Tn +
have$, and (3) $Tn + be$. (We shall return to the case of $Tn + V$
shortly.) The transformation then says to rewrite each of
these strings as follows:

Sentence 7.2b $Tn + can + the\ boy + go$
Sentence 7.3b $Tn + have + the\ boy + en + go$
Sentence 7.4b $Tn + be + the\ boy + ing + go$

If we assume that Tn is *Pres*, and if we apply the appropriate affix (flip-flop) transformations, we will get:

Sentence 7.2c $can + the\ boy + go$
Sentence 7.3c $has + the\ boy + gone$
Sentence 7.4c $is + the\ boy + going$

Each of these, of course, is a yes/no question. Branching tree diagrams for the deep and surface structures of Sentence 7.2 are given on the facing page.

Suppose, however, instead of *the boy*, we had expanded the nominal into a *wh-* plus a PRO form. This would give:

Sentence 7.5a $Q + wh\text{-} PRO_N + Tn + can + go$
Sentence 7.6a $Q + wh\text{-} PRO_N + Tn + have + en + go$
Sentence 7.7a $Q + wh\text{-} PRO_N + Tn + be + ing + go$

As before, the transformation says to replace $\{Q\}$ with the element containing Tn, giving:

Sentence 7.5b $Tn + can + wh\text{-} PRO_N + go$
Sentence 7.6b $Tn + have + wh\text{-} PRO_N + en + go$
Sentence 7.7b $Tn + be + wh\text{-} PRO_N + ing + go$

In this case, however, we do not get a yes/no question because we have a *wh-* present in the string. The rule says to move the element containing *wh-* to the first position in the string, giving:

Sentence 7.5c $wh\text{-} PRO_N + Tn + can + go$
Sentence 7.6c $wh\text{-} PRO_N + Tn + have + en + go$
Sentence 7.7c $wh\text{-} PRO_N + Tn + be + ing + go$

If we assume that the PRO form is animate, then these strings will produce:

Sentence 7.5d $who + can + go$
Sentence 7.6d $who + has + gone$
Sentence 7.7d $who + is + going$

This family of transformations is sufficiently important to warrant further examples. Suppose we wish to question the direct object of a transitive verb, as in the following examples:

Sentence 7.8a $Q + the\ boy + Tn + can + eat + wh\text{-} PRO_N$
Sentence 7.9a $Q + the\ boy + Tn + have + en + eat + wh\text{-}$
   PRO_N
Sentence 7.10a $Q + the\ boy + Tn + be + ing + eat + wh\text{-} PRO_N$

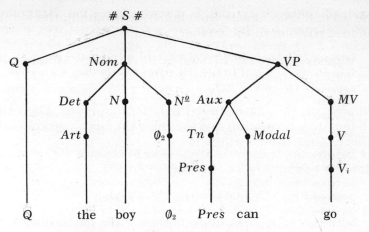

Figure 7.1   Sentence 7.2, deep structure.

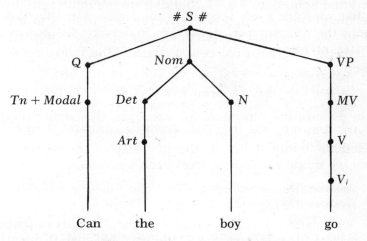

Figure 7.2   Sentence 7.2, surface structure.

The first step in the transformation replaces {Q} with the element containing *Tn*:

Sentence 7.8b $Tn + can + the\ boy + eat + wh\text{-}\ PRO_N$
Sentence 7.9b $Tn + have + the\ boy + en + eat + wh\text{-}\ PRO_N$
Sentence 7.10b $Tn + be + the\ boy + ing + eat + wh\text{-}\ PRO_N$

The second step moves the element containing the *wh-* to the first position in the string:

Sentence 7.8c $wh\text{-} PRO_N + Tn + can + the\ boy + eat$
Sentence 7.9c $wh\text{-} PRO_N + Tn + have + the\ boy + en + eat$
Sentence 7.10c $wh\text{-} PRO_N + Tn + be + the\ boy + ing + eat$

Suppose, in this case, that PRO_N is inanimate. Then the flip-flop transformation and the relevant morphographemic rules change these strings to:

Sentence 7.8d $what + can + the\ boy + eat$
Sentence 7.9d $what + has + the\ boy + eaten$
Sentence 7.10d $what + is + the\ boy + eating$

Sentences 7.2 − 7.4 illustrate the simple yes/no question; Sentences 7.5 − 7.7 illustrate the interrogation of the subject; and Sentences 7.8 − 7.10 illustrate the interrogation of the direct object. Suppose, however, we wished to interrogate an adverbial. In particular, suppose we wished to derive the interrogative counterpart of the following sentence:

Sentence 7.11 $the\ boy + can + leave + SOMETIME$

In a declarative sentence, for example, this string might lead to *The boy can leave today*. If, however, we had selected the optional {Q} in the first step of the derivation, then we might produce strings such as:

Sentence 7.12a $Q + the\ boy + Tn + can + leave + wh\text{-} TIME$
Sentence 7.13a $Q + the\ boy + Tn + have + en + leave +$
                 $wh\text{-} TIME$
Sentence 7.14a $Q + the\ boy + Tn + be + ing + leave + wh\text{-}$
                 $TIME$

The first step in the transformation replaces {Q} with the element containing Tn:

Sentence 7.12b $Tn + can + the\ boy + leave + wh\text{-} TIME$
Sentence 7.13b $Tn + have + the\ boy + en + leave + wh\text{-}$
                 $TIME$
Sentence 7.14b $Tn + be + the\ boy + ing + leave + wh\text{-} TIME$

The second step moves the element containing the *wh-* to the first position in the string:

Sentence 7.12c   *wh- TIME + Tn + can + the boy + leave*
Sentence 7.13c   *wh- TIME + Tn + have + the boy + en + leave*
Sentence 7.14c   *wh- TIME + Tn + be + the boy + ing + leave*

And these strings would produce:

Sentence 7.12d   *when + can + the boy + leave*
Sentence 7.13d   *when + has + the boy + left*
Sentence 7.14d   *when + is + the boy + leaving*

In short, this family of transformations automatically produces yes/no and *wh-* interrogatives from any string containing $\{Q\}$. Branching tree diagrams for the deep and surface structures of Sentence 7.12 are given on page 184.

But we have not yet considered the case in which the tense morpheme $\{Tn\}$ does not precede an auxiliary but rather precedes an intransitive, transitive, or copulative verb. That is, we have not yet considered the first line in the interrogative transformation:

$$Q + Nom + Tn + V \Longrightarrow Tn + Nom + V$$

If we are questioning the subject, that is, if the *Nom* in this string is expanded to *wh- PRO$_N$*, then our second rule applies and we move the element containing the *wh-* to the first position in the string. This will give *wh- PRO$_N$ + Tn + V*, which is a correct description of such sentences as:

Sentence 7.15   Who sleeps?
Sentence 7.16   Who saw the dog?
Sentence 7.17   What seems good?

That is, the first word in the string is automatically converted into an interrogative pronoun and the tense marker $\{Tn\}$ becomes attached to the main verb by the affix (flip-flop) transformation. But suppose we are not questioning the subject and that no auxiliary intervenes between the tense marker $\{Tn\}$ and $\{V\}$ (i.e., any V_i, V_t, V_c). This could result in two different strings, depending on whether or

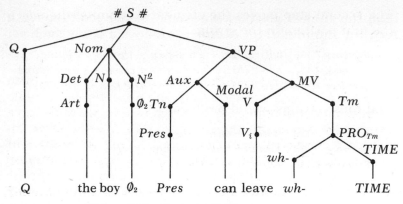

Figure 7.3   Sentence 7.12, deep structure.

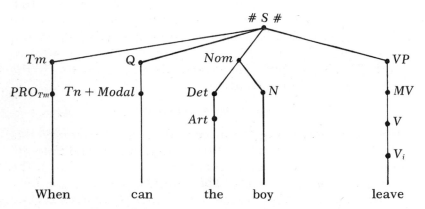

Figure 7.4   Sentence 7.12, surface structure.

not there is an occurrence of *wh-* in the matrix. If there is no occurrence of *wh-* then, obviously, there is no element containing a *wh-* to move to the first position of the sentence, and we would be left with the string given by the first step of the transformation, i.e.:

$$Tn + Nom + V$$

If, on the other hand, there is a *wh-* in some position other than the subject position, we would be obliged to move it forward and might, for example, produce a string such as:

$$wh\text{-} PRO_N + Tn + Nom + V$$

Notice that in both cases the symbol $\{Tn\}$ is isolated from the main verb and, consequently, the affix (flip-flop) transformation cannot apply. Obviously, however, we must have a verb as a carrier for the tense marker. We therefore introduce a transformation that replaces any occurrence of an isolated affix (including *Pres* and *Pas*) by a combination of *do* + *Af*. In other words, we introduce an obligatory auxiliary *to do* as a carrier of the isolated bound morpheme.[2]

Again, a few illustrations should clarify the matter. Suppose we have the following string:[3]

$$Q + Nom + Tn + V_t + Nom + Tm$$

This might underlie any of the following strings:

Sentence 7.18a $Q + wh\text{-} PRO_N + Pas + see + the\ dog + today$
Sentence 7.19a $Q + Mary + Pas + see + wh\text{-} PRO_N + today$
Sentence 7.20a $Q + Mary + Pas + see + the\ dog + wh\text{-} TIME$
Sentence 7.21a $Q + Mary + Pas + see + the\ dog + today$

Since Sentences 7.18−7.21 are all a case of $Q + Nom + Tn + V$, we must apply the interrogative transformation to produce:

Sentence 7.18b $Pas + wh\text{-} PRO_N + see + the\ dog + today$
Sentence 7.19b $Pas + Mary + see + wh\text{-} PRO_N + today$

---

[2] Somewhat more precisely, we may say that any time an affix is isolated between word boundary markers after applying the word boundary transformation, then we must replace the symbol *Af* by a combination of *do* + *Af*. Symbolically:

T 7.7 $\#Af\# \Longrightarrow \#do + Af\#$

[3] In this set of sentences, we introduce *Name* as an optional expansion of *Nom*; that is, we rewrite the PS rule which expands *Nom*:

PS 7.7 $Nom \longrightarrow \begin{Bmatrix} Det + N + N^{\underline{o}} \\ Name \end{Bmatrix} (+S)$

(See Figures 7.5 and 7.6)

Sentence 7.20b　　$Pas + Mary + see + the\ dog + wh\text{-}\ TIME$

Sentence 7.21b　　$Pas + Mary + see + the\ dog + today$

The second step of the transformation then moves any element containing a *wh-* to the first position in the sentence. Obviously, this applies only to Sentences 7.18b – 7.20b; it does not affect Sentence 7.21b, since there is no occurrence of a *wh-*. Thus we have:

Sentence 7.18c　　$wh\text{-}\ PRO_N + Pas + see + the\ dog + today$

Sentence 7.19c　　$wh\text{-}\ PRO_N + Pas + Mary + see + today$

Sentence 7.20c　　$wh\text{-}\ TIME + Pas + Mary + see + the\ dog$

Sentence 7.21c　　$Pas + Mary + see + the\ dog + today$

We then apply the *do* transformation to every isolated case of $\{Tn\}$ (in this case, *Pas*). Notice that this transformation does not apply to Sentence 7.18c since *Pas* is not isolated but is rather followed by V_t:

Sentence 7.18d　　$wh\text{-}\ PRO_N + Pas + see + the\ dog + today$

Sentence 7.19d　　$wh\text{-}\ PRO_N + do + Pas + Mary + see + today$

Sentence 7.20d　　$wh\text{-}\ TIME + do + Pas + Mary + see + the\ dog$

Sentence 7.21d　　$do + Pas + Mary + see + the\ dog + today$

These strings, in turn, underlie the sentences:

Sentence 7.18e　　Who saw the dog today?

Sentence 7.19e　　What did Mary see today?

Sentence 7.20e　　When did Mary see the dog?

Sentence 7.21e　　Did Mary see the dog today?

Branching tree diagrams for the deep and surface structures of Sentence 7.19 are given on the facing page.

When combined with the obligatory *do* transformation, the interrogative transformation is obviously one of the most powerful transformations in all of English grammar. It also fits perfectly with the embedding transformation.

To summarize, the interrogative transformation performs the following functions: It moves the tense marker (and the first auxiliary if one or more auxiliaries are present) to the first position in the derivational string where it

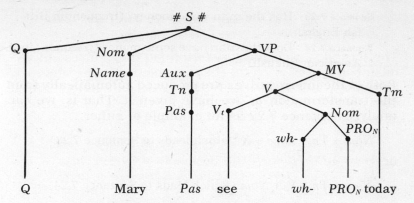

Figure 7.5   Sentence 7.19, deep structure.

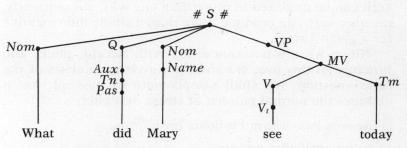

Figure 7.6   Sentence 7.19, surface structure.

replaces the interrogative morpheme {Q}. The *wh-* transformation then applies (and this is the same transformation that applies to any *wh-* including those in constituent
sentences); specifically, the *wh-* transformation moves any
element containing a *wh-* to the front of its string (either
matrix or constituent). Then, if required, the *do* transformation applies to attach any isolated affix to the carrier *do*.

   There is one interesting fact about interrogative sentences in which the verb *to have* is used as a main verb.
Notice the following sentences:

Sentence 7.22   The man has some money.

Sentence 7.23 Has the man some money? (frequent in British English)

Sentence 7.24 Does the man have some money? (frequent in American English)

Both of the interrogatives are produced automatically from the transformation as we have given it. That is, we can analyze Sentence 7.22 as an example of either

$$Nom + Tn + have + X \text{ (which leads to Sentence 7.23)}$$

or

$$Nom + Tn + V_t + Nom \text{ (which leads to Sentence 7.24)}$$

And since the sentence can be analyzed in two ways, it produces two interrogative forms automatically. No other verb can be analyzed in more than one way; consequently, no other verb can produce more than a single interrogative for a given string.

Since we are not concerned with accent, pitch, and juncture in this text, we shall not give an analysis of the echo question. We shall simply note in passing that it changes the normal pattern of stress and pitch

Sentence 7.25 The girl is doing her h^o^{m}e$_w$$_o$$_r$$_k$.

to an interrogative pattern

Sentence 7.25a The girl is doing her home^w^{o}^{r}^{k}?

We can, however, look briefly at the transformation which produces tag questions.

Briefly, this transformation uses the same structural analysis as the regular interrogative transformation. But instead of replacing {Q} with the tense marker (and the first auxiliary if there is one or more), the transformation (1) adds a duplicate tense marker (and a duplicate of the first auxiliary if there is one or more) following the sentence; (2) adds a PRO form of the same number and gender as the subject after the duplicate tense marker (and any duplicate auxiliary); (3) adds {-n't} to the duplicate tense marker if there is no negative morpheme present in the matrix sentence; (4) and, finally, deletes the {Q}. These steps are shown in the following derivations:

Sentence 7.26   *Q + the boy + Pres + have + en + go*
Sentence 7.27   *Q + the boy + Pas + go*
Sentence 7.28   *Q + the boy + Pres + have + -n't + en + go*

The first step of the transformation adds the duplicate tense marker (and a duplicate of the first auxiliary if there is one or more):

Sentence 7.26a   *Q + the boy + Pres + have + en + go + Pres + have*
Sentence 7.27a   *Q + the boy + Pas + go + Pas*
Sentence 7.28a   *Q + the boy + Pres + have + -n't + en + go + Pres + have*

Then the transformation adds a PRO form of the same number and gender of the subject:

Sentence 7.26b   *Q + the boy + Pres + have + en + go + Pres + have + he*
Sentence 7.27b   *Q + the boy + Pas + go + Pas + he*
Sentence 7.28b   *Q + the boy + Pres + have + -n't + en + go + Pres + have + he*

As a third step, the transformation adds {-*n't*} to the duplicate tense marker if there is no negative preverb present in the matrix sentence (that is, in this case, to Sentences 7.26b and 7.27b):

Sentence 7.26c   *Q + the boy + Pres + have + en + go + Pres + have + -n't + he*
Sentence 7.27c   *Q + the boy + Pas + go + Pas + -n't + he*
Sentence 7.28c   *Q + the boy + Pres + have + -n't + en + go + Pres + have + he*

Then the transformation deletes the {Q}:

Sentence 7.26d   *the boy + Pres + have + en + go + Pres + have + n't + he*
Sentence 7.27d   *the boy + Pas + go + Pas + -n't + he*
Sentence 7.28d   *the boy + Pres + have + -n't + en + go + Pres + have + he*

The affix transformation and the appropriate morphographemic rules will turn Sentences 7.26d and 7.28d into:

Sentence 7.26e   The boy has gone, hasn't he?
Sentence 7.28e   The boy hasn't gone, has he?

But notice that in Sentence 7.27d, we have an isolated affix: *Pas*. The affix cannot remain isolated, so we must apply the *do* transformation to get:

Sentence 7.27e   *the boy + Pas + go + do + Pas + -n't + he*

We may now apply the affix transformation and the appropriate morphographemic rules to get:

Sentence 7.27f   The boy went, didn't he?

7.2   NEGATIVE AND EMPHATIC SENTENCES

Once again we have evidence of how systematic the rules of English are. We introduced the *do* transformation to take care of those cases in which an isolated affix occurred in regular interrogatives, and we find that the same transformation also accounts for any isolated affix that occurs in tag questions. But the system is even more efficient than these two examples indicate. Consider the case in which we select the presentence element {*Ng*} but do not select an auxiliary verb. After the appropriate transformations and morphographemic rules have been applied, we might get a string such as:

Sentence 7.29   *the boy + Pas + Ng + go*

The presence of the negative morpheme in this string prohibits the operation of the affix (flip-flop) transformation and leaves us with an isolated affix. Consequently, we apply the *do* transformation to get:

Sentence 7.29a   *the boy + do + Pas + Ng + go*

And we may then apply additional morphographemic rules to get:

Sentence 7.29b   The boy didn't go.

There is one additional case in which we must apply the obligatory *do* transformation. Consider the following sentences:

Sentence 7.30a   The boy has gone to the store.
Sentence 7.30b   The boy *has* gone to the store.

Sentence 7.30b is more emphatic than Sentence 7.30a. To account for this, we can postulate the existence of an emphatic morpheme {*Emph*}, which, like the {*Q*} and {*Ng*} morphemes, is an optional element introduced into the first phrase-structure rule:

PS 7.1b $S \longrightarrow (Ng) (Emph) (Q) Nom + VP$

Suppose we optionally select {*Emph*} and not {*Q*} or {*Ng*}. We might then produce a string such as:

Sentence 7.30c   *Emph + the boy + Pres + have + en + go + to the store*

The emphatic transformation shifts the {*Emph*} to a position behind the tense marker and the first auxiliary (if there are one or more auxiliaries) or behind the tense marker if there is no auxiliary. Then we would get:

Sentence 7.30d   *the boy + Pres + have + Emph + en + go + to the store*

Sentence 7.30e   *the boy + has + Emph + gone + to the store*

And a morphographemic rule would indicate that any word followed by {*Emph*} is to be indicated in print by italics:

Sentence 7.30f   The boy *has* gone to the store.

If there were no auxiliary verb present in the derivation, however, we would get:

Sentence 7.30g   *Emph + the boy + Pas + go + to the store*

The emphatic transformation would move the {*Emph*} to a position immediately following the tense marker:

Sentence 7.30h   *the boy + Pas + Emph + go + to the store*

And again we have a case of an isolated affix, which brings

the *do* transformation into play, giving:

Sentence 7.30i   *the boy + do + Pas + Emph + go + to the store*

And the morphographemic rules change this to:

Sentence 7.30j   The boy *did* go to the store.

7.3 PASSIVE VOICE

There is still some debate among transformational linguists as to the best method of introducing the passive
morpheme {*by + Psv*} into the phrase-structure rules. For
our purposes, we can assume that it is introduced optionally after any regular transitive verb (but not after any
middle verb). We might, therefore, derive a string such as
the following:

Sentence 7.31   *the boy + Pres + have + en + buy + by + Psv
+ the car*

The transformation that applies to strings like this operates
in three steps: (1) it replaces the symbol *Psv* with the first
nominal; (2) it moves the direct object into the position
formerly occupied by the subject; and (3) it introduces *be
+ en* after the auxiliaries and before the main verb. Thus,
in three steps, we have:

Sentence 7.31a   *+ Pres + have + en + buy + by + the boy +
the car*

Sentence 7.31b   *the car + Pres + have + en + buy + by +
the boy*

Sentence 7.31c   *the car + Pres + have + en + be + en + buy
+ by + the boy*

After applying the affix transformation and the relevant
morphographemic rules, we have:

Sentence 7.31d   The car has been bought by the boy.

Optionally, and as a fourth step, we may delete the combination of *by plus the original subject.* This would give:

Sentence 7.31e   The car has been bought.

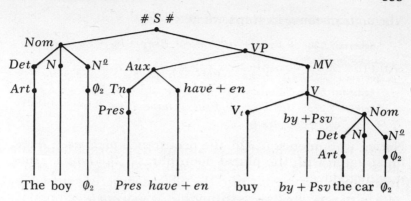

Figure 7.7   Sentence 7.31, deep structure.

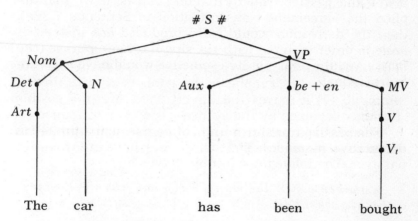

Figure 7.8   Sentence 7.31, surface structure.

Branching tree diagrams for the deep and surface structures of Sentence 7.31 are given above.

There is one restriction on this transformation: it must be applied *before* the transformation that guarantees agreement between the subject and the verb. Consider the following case:

Sentence 7.32a   *the man + Pres + have + en + see + by + Psv + the boys*

Again, proceeding in steps we get:

Sentence 7.32b $+ Pres + have + en + see + by + the\ man +$
the boys

Sentence 7.32c $the\ boys + Pres + have + en + see + by +$
the man

Sentence 7.32d $the\ boys + Pres + have + en + be + en +$
$see + by + the\ man$

Notice in Sentence 7.32d the occurrence of *Pres + have*
must agree with the plural noun phrase (*the boys*). Thus
it will produce:

Sentence 7.32e   The boys have been seen by the man.

If we had applied the agreement transformation *before* applying the passive transformation (that is, if we had applied the agreement transformation to Sentence 7.32a),
then the derivation would have produced *has* instead of
have in order to agree with the singular noun phrase (*the
man*). And the final, passive sentence would have been ungrammatical:

*The boys has been seen by the man.

The passive transformation, of course, is not limited to
declarative sentences. That is, we may have interrogative
passives. The following example is typical:

Sentence 7.33a $Q + the\ man + Pas + buy + by + Psv + the$
$car + wh\text{-}\ TIME$

The passive transformation produces (in three steps):

Sentence 7.33b $Q + Pas + buy + by + the\ man + the\ car +$
$wh\text{-}\ TIME$

Sentence 7.33c $Q + the\ car + Pas + buy + by + the\ man +$
$wh\text{-}\ TIME$

Sentence 7.33d $Q + the\ car + Pas + be + en + buy + by +$
$the\ man + wh\text{-}\ TIME$

The interrogative transformation then replaces the {Q}
with the tense marker and the following auxiliary to produce:

Sentence 7.33e *Pas + be + the car + en + buy + by + the man + wh- TIME*

And the *wh-* transformation moves the element containing the *wh-* to the front of the string:

Sentence 7.33f *wh- TIME + Pas + be + the car + en + buy + by + the man*

We then apply the flip-flop transformation, the *be + Pas* transformation and, finally, the morphographemic rules to produce:

Sentence 7.33g When was the car bought by the man?

We should also note that the passive transformation can apply either to the direct object or to the indirect object. Thus, for an active voice sentence such as:

Sentence 7.34 The man gave some money to the boy.

We can produce the following passives:

Sentence 7.34a Some money was given to the boy by the man.
Sentence 7.34b Some money was given to the boy.
Sentence 7.34c The boy was given some money by the man.
Sentence 7.34d The boy was given some money.

(Notice that we must include a direction to drop the *to* when the indirect object is moved to the subject position.) This transformation—combined with the Q and *wh-* transformations—will also produce:

Sentence 7.34e Who was given some money?

In the case of the interrogative, however, we have the option of retaining the *to* that marks the indirect object; we also have an optional placement for the direct object:

Sentence 7.34f To whom was some money given?
Sentence 7.34g Who was some money given to? (colloquial, but increasingly common)

Although we shall not do so here, it is relatively easy to

adjust the transformation to produce these variants in an interrogative passive sentence.

7.4 IMPERATIVES

The imperative transformation is quite simple. It operates only on strings that have (1) a second-person pronoun in the subject position, (2) a present tense marker, (3) the auxiliary *will*, and (4) no other auxiliaries. The following string is typical of those that meet these qualifications.

Sentence 7.35 $PRO_{N_2} + Pres + will + close + the\ door.$

(Here the PRO_{N_2} indicates the second person pronoun *you*.) The transformation deletes the subject, the tense marker, and the auxiliary to give:

Sentence 7.35a   *close + the door*

And the morphographemic rules give:

Sentence 7.35b   Close the door!

Alternatively, there is another transformation that retains the subject (i.e., PRO_{N_2}) but deletes the tense marker and the auxiliary to give ultimately:

Sentence 7.35c   You, close the door!

Notice that we can also apply the tag-question transformation to this derivation. Since the auxiliary, to which {Ng} would normally be attached, is deleted in the transformation, we have the alternative of both positive and negative tags:

Sentence 7.35d $close + the\ door + Pres + will + PRO_{N_2}$
Sentence 7.35e $close + the\ door + Pres + will + \text{-}n't + PRO_{N_2}$

These give, respectively:

Sentence 7.35f   Close the door, will you?
Sentence 7.35g   Close the door, won't you?

Finally, we should also note that we can embed a constituent sentence after the subject nominal. Thus, we might have:

Sentence 7.35h PRO_{N_2} (+S) + *Pres* + *will* + *close* + *the door*

And we might expand the constituent as follows:

Sentence 7.35i PRO_{N_2} (+PRO_{N_2} + *Pres* + *be* + *John*) + *Pres* + *will* + *close* + *the door*

The word *John* is then in apposition to the subject nominal, and will lead to either of the following strings (depending upon whether or not we delete the PRO_{N_2} subject):

Sentence 7.35j   You, John, close the door!
Sentence 7.35k   John, close the door!

And to go one more step, we could add the tag-question transformation to produce:

Sentence 7.35l   John, close the door, will you?

Or, instead of the tag, we could add the negative morpheme (which would automatically trigger the *do* transformation):

Sentence 7.35m   John, don't close the door!

Again we see that various combinations of simple transformations can account for all the complexities of sentences.

7.5   SHOES AND SHIPS AND SEALING WAX

Before turning, in the final chapter, to some observations on the place of transformational grammar in the schools, we must look first at some miscellaneous topics that we have passed over in earlier chapters. Because we have lacked space for a more exhaustive presentation and because some of the topics have not yet been the subject of detailed investigation, we have had little to say about **conjunctions**, the source of **genitives**, the **subjunctive mood**, and the varieties of **prepositions**. In the next few pages, we shall look at each of these briefly.

Conjunctions. School grammars, for good reason, tend to be obscure in discussing conjunctions. They are certainly structure words but they can also function as form words. The only example of a pure coordinating conjunction is *and*. The other so-called coordinating conjunctions (e.g., *but, or, nor, for*) are all limited in one or more ways. Only rarely, for example, can we join two subject nominals with *but*:

> Sentence 7.36   John and Mary came.
> *John but Mary came.

And the subordinating conjunctions are even more confusing.

We can easily account for the so-called subordinating conjunctive adverbs (e.g., *when, whenever, where, whereever, while, why* and so on) by extending the *wh-* transformation to include adverbials. Consider the following sentences:

> Sentence 7.37a   I will go *SOMETIME* (+S). (matrix)
> Sentence 7.37b   I am ready *SOMETIME*. (constituent)

We can replace the PRO form in the constituent with *wh-Time*. The *wh-* transformation then moves it forward in its string. We then insert it as a constituent into the matrix, and finally delete the matrix PRO form:

> Sentence 7.37c   I will go *SOMETIME* (*wh- TIME* I am ready).
> Sentence 7.37d   I will go when I am ready.

The exact details have yet to be worked out, but it seems to the author that there is a connection between certain pairs of words: *when* and *after* (Sentence 7.38), *why* and *because* (Sentence 7.39), *whether* and *if* (Sentence 7.40), and so on. Consequently, there is probably a non-*wh* transformation that corresponds to the *wh-* transformation:

> Sentence 7.38a   He came when we were ready to leave.
> Sentence 7.38b   He came after we were ready to leave.

Sentence **7.39a**   I know he was there for *SOME REASON* (+S). (matrix)

Sentence **7.39b**   *SOME REASON* is *SOMETHING* (+S) (first constituent)

Sentence **7.39c**   I saw him. (second constituent)

Sentence **7.39d**   *SOME REASON* is (that I saw him) (new first constituent)

Sentence **7.39e**   I know he was there for *SOME REASON* (*SOME REASON* is that I saw him) (new matrix)

Sentence **7.39f**   I know he is there because I saw him. (derived sentence)

Sentence **7.40a**   I don't know whether I will go.

Sentence **7.40b**   I don't know if I will go.

We can say, however, that all conjunctions, that is, both subordinating and coordinating, are introduced into a matrix sentence from a constituent.

Genitives.   The author, for one, is not satisfied with the analyses of genitives that have been published. At present, some linguists suggest that genitives are derived by nominalizing sentences with *to have* as a main verb:

Sentence **7.41**   *The boy has a bike.* $\Longrightarrow$ *The boy's bike . . .*

Sentence **7.42**   *The table has a leg.* $\Longrightarrow$ *The leg of the table*

. . .

This nominalization accounts for most genitives of possession, but not all. For example, we cannot say:

*The man has a rudeness.

However, we can say:

The man's rudeness . . .

And the nominalization does not account for the ambiguity inherent in an expression such as *The king's picture . . .* which could mean either "The picture that belongs to the king" or "The artistic reproduction of the king's likeness."[4]

---

[4] Possibly the latter (the *likeness*) interpretation may be derived from an obligatory nominalization: *Someone pictured the king. $\Longrightarrow$ Someone's picture of the king . . . $\Longrightarrow$ the king's picture. . . .*

Furthermore, the nominalization will not produce the so-called **genitives of measure** or all of the **genitives of origin**. The following are not acceptable:

*The work has an hour.   *Nestle has chocolate.

However, these phrases are:

The hour's work . . .   Nestle's chocolate . . .

The analysis of genitives is also confused by the fact that some genitives are introduced into the grammar by expanding the phrase-structure rule for postdeterminers. In short, some progress toward understanding the operation of genitives has been made, but much more analysis is needed.

Subjunctive Mood.   The subjunctive mood is rapidly disappearing in modern English except in a few, well-established phrases such as *God bless America!* The reason is fairly simple: most of the subjunctive forms are identical to those of the indicative. The only differences (excluding, as usual, the verb *to be*) occur in the third-person singular of the present tense which, in the subjunctive, lacks the {-s} morpheme, and in the very unusual present progressive subjunctive where the verb *to be* is uninflected:

I be coming   we be coming
you be coming   you be coming
he be coming   they be coming

The grammar would indicate that such verbs as *prefer, suggest,* and *insist* may be followed by factive nominals in which the verb is in the subjunctive mood (*I prefer that Roger go. The committee suggests that you be here by nine o'clock. We insisted that Phyllis come with us.*).

Prepositions.   Finally, we have throughout the text simply assumed that a detailed analysis of English prepositions exists. This, unfortunately, is not true. Such an analysis will probably show that certain prepositions invariably occur with certain kinds of adverbials. Most prepositions, however, occur with more than one kind of adverbial: *He lives at home (Loc)* and *He came at four o'clock (Tm)*. A few words called prepositions seem to serve as markers or identifying morphemes of some sort: for example, the indirect object may be marked by *to*, and the genitive may be marked by *of* as in *the picture of the king*.

It is also very difficult to classify such words as *with* in phrases like the following: *The man with the beard* . . . and *Having worked with children* . . . . And certainly it is wrong to consider the *of* that occurs with predeterminers as a preposition. Consider:

> Sentence 7.43a The men are going.
>
> Sentence 7.43b All of the men are going.

The logical subject in each of these sentences is obviously *men*, but if we say that *of* is simply a preposition in Sentence 7.43b then we are somehow separating *All* and *of the men*. The author agrees with the majority of transformational linguists who feel that the separation should be *All of* and *the men*.

A similar situation arises with nouns of quantity. Certainly *prevention* and *cure* are not logically subordinate in the aphorism:

> Sentence 7.44 An ounce of prevention is worth a pound of cure.

But these distinctions are not yet completely understood. This fact underscores a point that has been made, implicitly and explicitly, throughout the text: like every other grammar, transformational grammar is incomplete. And as in every other field of humanistic inquiry, there is still work to be done.

7.6 SUMMARY

This chapter has had two purposes: (1) to present that part of current transformational theory that relates to variations on the basic pattern of active, declarative, indicative sentences, and (2) to indicate some of the areas of grammar that remain to be studied. In the first part of the chapter we saw that there are well-defined rules for deriving interrogatives, passives, and imperatives from kernel sentences. We saw, further, that various combinations of transformations and optional morphemes can be combined to produce the complex sentences that make up the vast majority of written English as well as a large part of spoken English. In the latter part of the chapter we noticed briefly that some aspects of transformational analysis seem incomplete (for example, the analysis of prepositions) and some few aspects even seem faulty (for example, the analysis of genitives). But these omissions and mistakes are not sufficient reason to dismiss transformational grammar any more than a physicist would discard modern physics because it fails to account fully for the phenomenon of light.

Discussion

1. In the text we noted that there are several kinds of interrogatives in Modern English: (1) regular yes/no questions, (2) *wh-* questions, (3) tag questions, and (4) echo questions. Consult some passages of dialogue in an eighteenth-century novel, a Shakespearean play, a tale from Chaucer, and *Beowulf*. Do you find the same variety? What kinds of questions predominate? Can you find kinds of questions that no longer exist in Modern English (*cf.*, Thackeray, *The Rose and the Ring*: "Runs not a river by my palace wall?")?

2. Sentences 7.23 and 7.24 reflect one of the differences between British and American English. What other differences can you discover? How do such differences develop? Can we say that either the British or the American form is more correct? Why?

3. Consult the discussion of "stress," "pitch," and "juncture" in such a textbook as James Sledd's *A Short Intro-*

duction to English Grammar. What kinds of rules would be required to incorporate these "suprasegmentals" into a transformational grammar of English? What relationship would exist between these rules and the commas that we have inserted in the appositive transformation? and the question mark (?) that follows an interrogative sentence? and the emphatic transformation?

4. In the text we have been concerned only with those negatives that precede verbs. Where else can negatives occur in sentences? What relationship do these other negatives have to those that precede verbs? What does this suggest about rules that restrict the co-occurrence of negatives in Modern English? How do the modern rules on the occurrence of negatives compare with those that were current in Shakespeare's time? Compare the occurrence of negatives in English with those of another Indo-European language.

5. In the text we discussed some of the limitations that restrict the occurrence of the conjunctions *but, or, nor* and *for.* What are some other limitations? How do these conjunctions compare with the so-called subordinating conjunctions (e.g., *if, although*)?

6. Transformational grammar, like all grammars, is incomplete. How does this affect the usefulness of the grammar for the teacher of English? What are the advantages and disadvantages of telling a student that every book about grammar is necessarily incomplete? What, in your opinion, are the major weaknesses of transformational grammar? Can these weaknesses be overcome? How (or, if more appropriate, why not)?

Exercises

1. Using PS 7.1 (p. 178) and the interrogative transformation in conjunction with the rules in the fourth model grammar (p. 140), derive the following sentences:

  1. Can the child dance today?
  2. Has the monster seen the children?
  3. Is the man sleeping?

2. Using Figure 7.1 and Figure 7.2 as models, construct branching tree diagrams for the sentences in Exercise 1.

3. Select a paragraph each from a newspaper, a modern novel, and a textbook. Mark the occurrence of each of the following transformations: agreement (i.e., T 5.1), affix, adjective, relative clause, yes/no interrogative, *wh-* interrogative, imperative, emphatic, passive.

4. Select any five kernel sentences and, without going through the derivations, reorder them by performing the following transformations: adjective, relative clause, yes/no interrogative, *wh-* interrogative, emphatic, and (where possible) passive. For example:

  1. The man will build a boat tomorrow. (kernel)
  2. The handsome man will build a boat tomorrow. (*adj*)
  3. The man who lives next door will build a boat tomorrow. (relative)
  4. Will the man build a boat tomorrow? (yes/no)
  5. When will the man build a boat? (*wh-*)
  6. The man *will* build a boat tomorrow. (*Emph*)
  7. A boat will be built (by the man) tomorrow. (*pass*)

5. Use the sentences of Exercise 4 and reorder them by performing as many of the transformations as possible for each sentence. For example:

  1. When *will* a boat be built by the handsome man who lives next door? (*wh-, emph, pass, adj, relative*)

⟨8⟩

Grammar and the School

How haughtily he cocks his nose,
To tell what every schoolboy knows.

SWIFT, *The Country Life.*

As teachers of English, we have two primary aims: we want to explain the nature of language to our pupils, and we want, if possible, to instill in them some awareness of the humanistic values that inhere in the study of literature. A knowledge of grammar can obviously help us to achieve the first aim, particularly if this knowledge is based upon a coherent and viable philosophy for teaching the English language arts. Somewhat less obviously, but nonetheless certainly, a knowledge of grammar can also help us to achieve the second aim. This final and frankly polemical chapter discusses these two aims, argues for a new philosophy, and suggests some of the ways that a knowledge of grammar applies to the understanding and appreciation of literature.

8.1 A NEW PHILOSOPHY

For various reasons that are part of the fabric of the American educational system and its history, the English language arts are wondrously fragmented, so much so that they have not been encompassed by a single, meaningful, and coherent philosophy. We flirt with the new while pledging fidelity to the old; we embrace bits and pieces of mu-

205

tually antagonistic philosophies; and we fondly ignore the vital and potentially productive distinction between theory and practice. The fragmentation is worse than debilitating: it is genuinely destructive. If the English language arts are to have significance and meaning for our students, we must put an end to fragmentation. We must develop a basic, flexible, viable philosophy.

What facts do we know that can serve to inform such a philosophy? Most importantly, we know that every normal child, even a child in kindergarten, produces hundreds of English sentences every day. The vast majority of these sentences are perfectly formed; only a very small minority are so structurally misshapen as to be unintelligible.

We also know that many of these sentences are totally new. The child has never heard them before. In other words, by the age of six the normal child is able to create sentences; he has long since abandoned the notion of speech-as-repetition which is common in children at the age of two or three. This means, of course, that a child of six has a grammar, i.e., "a device for producing sentences." The grammar is certainly not complete, and we—as teachers—must guide its growth. But it is far more complete than we had ever realized or even suspected.

For the English language arts, then, this fact is basic: the child of six has a grammar. What other facts do we need to know? There are two important negative answers to this question. We do *not* need to know all the facts and theories of linguistics. We do *not* need to know all the facts relating to how a child first learns language.

Theories of linguistics are certainly important, and the writers of textbooks need to be familiar with them. On the other hand, the teacher does not need to be a linguistic theorist any more than he needs to be a mathematical or musical theorist. While preparing for certification, the typical teacher can learn enough about linguistics to be able to evaluate the textbooks he must use (and no textbook is perfect), and to be able to answer the typical questions that students raise. For example, a teacher should be able to distinguish those textbook rules that are based on syntax, and are therefore objective, from those that are based on usage, and are therefore a matter of subjective judgment. If a student asks why we introduce the word *do* in some negative sentences, the teacher should be able to answer that, in English, there is a syntactic rule which says that the negative must always follow or be attached to an auxiliary verb. But it would be folly to expect a teacher to be familiar with the fine points of the current linguistic argument about the nature of the verb *to be.* There are many times in a teacher's professional life when he must say, "I don't know." No man since the renaissance has been idealistic or naive enough to take all knowledge for his province.

The problem of how a child learns language, which is technically known as the problem of language acquisition, is a fascinating one for both psychologists and teachers. But as we noted in Chapter 1, even the most recent and exhaustive theory of language acquisition has been proved wrong,[1] and most psychologists are frank in admitting that the process is still a mystery. Certainly it would be helpful to know something of the process, but such knowledge is not a *sine qua non* for developing a philosophy for teaching the language arts.

But there are also some positive answers to the question of what facts we need to know. In particular, we need to know how much a child really knows about language by the age of six, how much we can profitably teach in any given school year, and how much a child should know at any particular age. We also need to know where to begin teaching language and what sequential steps are the most logical to follow. And finally, we need to know why we are teaching language at all.

The last question needs to be answered first.

In the opinion of the author, there are two separate but complementary reasons that justify the study and teaching

---

[1] Noam Chomsky, Review of B. F. Skinner's *Verbal Behavior*, in *Language*, XXXV, (January–March 1959), pp. 26–58.

of these arts. The first is humanistic; the second, pragmatic. Language is the most human, the most basic of all man's activities and accomplishments. This fact, in itself, is sufficient justification for the study of language. But there is also a practical justification. As we study language, we become increasingly aware of the broad resources that every speaker of every language possesses. Equally important, we also develop increasing self-confidence in our ability to use language. In sum, we should teach language, first, because it is important in itself, and second, because the proper study of language can increase our self-confidence in speaking, reading, writing, and listening.

There are, at present, few answers to the other questions.[2] During the coming decade we need to undertake large-scale research programs to discover these answers. What does a child know at the age of six? Is the syntactic knowledge of a child from one part of the country different from that of a child from another part? How much can we teach in a given school year? Can we teach best through discovery? Should the syntactic structure of the language used in textbooks bear a strong resemblance to the structure that a child uses at a given age? Can we teach certain facts about language before a child learns to read (as set theory is sometimes taught before simple addition in arithmetic classes)? What is the best way to group language facts together? For example, should we teach all the varieties of adverbs at the same time or should we teach adverbs of manner when we are teaching transitive verbs? These are vital questions that we must answer to improve our teaching. And answering them obviously requires the cooperation of experienced teachers.

These questions all relate to the student. We are in a better position when we ask questions about the subject matter. We know that linguists have made great strides in

---

[2] Kellogg W. Hunt, of Florida State, has been working through Project English to determine the kinds of transformations that children use at various ages. His study, though incomplete, is extremely important and revealing.

the analysis of language. They have, without doubt, provided us with more facts and information about language in the past fifty years than all the philosophers and philologists of the preceding five hundred years. Yet few of these facts are to be found in the so-called school grammars.

We also know that there is no need to discard traditional grammar as useless. Far from it. We want, rather, to build upon the theoretical foundation of traditional grammar, and at the same time we want to incorporate many of its terms and practical applications. We want, in short, to build much of traditional grammar into any complete philosophy of the English language arts.

What, then, should this philosophy be? On the basis of the aims we have and the facts we know, the author makes the following proposal:

> *The English language arts should be firmly based on the axiom that the vast majority of children intuitively know the fundamental structure of their language before they begin their formal education.*

This is the most important axiom, but there are several corrolaries that are only slightly less important:

1. A child should study *language* rather than grammar.
2. The ideal form of study is *discovery* rather than memorization.
3. The end result of the discovery procedure should be increased *self-confidence*.
4. Self-confidence is best developed through *sequentially ordered instruction*.

Obviously, it will take many years before the full effect of these proposals is felt in the schools. But there are several places where we can begin.

In the very early grades we can begin by rewriting the preprimers, primers, and readers so that the sentence patterns conform more closely to those that exist in the living language. At present, they conform neither to the patterns that are commonly used by children, nor to those that are typical in the speech or writing of educated adults. That is, most children have never heard – and will never read or hear outside the elementary grades – sentences that have syntactic patterns similar to those found in most readers. Writers of these books have long had available to them lists that give the frequency of particular words. We need now to compile lists of sentence and phrase patterns. More importantly, we need to avoid many of the artificial patterns that appear in practically all early readers. We are, in effect, forcing a young child to learn not only how to recognize words on a page but – at the same time – to derive sentence meanings from artificial and probably useless sentence patterns.

These facts can be proved simply by citing some typical examples from widely used readers:

Sentence 8.1   Is Bill here? Is Bill at home?

In many dialects of American English, the construction *at home* is rare, at least in speech. Most speakers and writers do not use the preposition *at* before the word *home*. The child has probably said "Is Bill home?" scores of times in his short life. He knows what the sentence means. Why should we force him to learn an artificially "correct" form (which is really no more correct than the other) when we are also trying to teach him to read? This example of false correctness is contradicted almost daily in the experience of the child and may lead him to conclude that there is a difference between "book language" and the language of daily life. Such a conclusion could adversely affect his entire educational life.

Sentence 8.2   Tom sees something big.

In one primer, this construction is the first use of an adjective. As we have seen in Chapter 6, it is rare in English that single-word adjectives follow the nouns they modify. Most of the adjectives that a child has heard have preceded the nouns they modify; he may not even know that adjectives usually follow indefinite pronouns such as *something* and *someone*. As a minimum requirement, we need to know more about children's language before writing primers and readers.

Sentence 8.3   You cannot go. You are not ready.

Children are certainly familiar with negatives; they are among the very first words they learn. But they are not familiar with the syntactic construction of sentences like Sentence 8.3. Most speakers and writers will rarely use the free morpheme {*not*} when they can use a contraction. They will say, instead: "You can't go. You aren't ready." Admittedly, these words look more complicated on the page because of the presence of the apostrophe. But they are a familiar part of the child's linguistic experience, whereas Sentence 8.3 is, at best, rare.

The sentences become even more awkward and unusual when they get longer:

Sentence 8.4   My father has put something in here.

Here the writer has used the present perfect tense rather than the simple past although young children use the simple past much more frequently. In fact, the use of the perfect with the verb *to put* is uncommon even in the speech of adults. Depending on the context, many speakers would say *My father put something in here*.

Perhaps the most common difference between the speech patterns of children and the sentence patterns found in primers and early readers is one that we have already noticed but which deserves more comment: the frequency of contractions in speech and the almost total absence of them in textbooks.

Sentence 8.5   It is in the house.
Sentence 8.6   I will go home. I will paint the chair.
Sentence 8.7   We are happy to go.
Sentence 8.8   Bill is not ready to go.

It seems most probable that children must learn to "translate" these supposedly regular patterns (which are rare in speech and even uncommon in informal writing) into patterns which they are familiar with and which are a familiar

part of their own linguistic experience: *It's, I'll, We're, isn't.*
Speaking linguistically, the contraction is no better or
worse than the uncontracted form. That is, there is nothing
"sloppy" about *it's* and nothing uniquely "correct" about
it is. On the other hand, and speaking statistically, the contraction is far more common than the uncontracted form.

We have also noticed that, in English, we tend to delete—or replace with PRO forms—repeated words and
phrases. Children do the same thing, of course. There are
certainly good pedagogical reasons for repeating words
that a child is learning, but we must weigh this advantage
against the rarity of such things in the child's linguistic
experience. We must, in particular, avoid giving the impression of two distinct languages: one for school and one
for the "real world."[3] Consider the following series of
sentences:

> Sentence 8.9   I see the kitten. I will get the white kitten.
>   Come here, little kitten.

The uncontracted sentence, of course, is rare in a child's
speech, but what is even more rare in Sentence 8.9 is the
total absence of pronouns. Normally, any child would say
"I'll get it." He knows what such a sentence means because
he uses sentences like it frequently. We can compare the
difference between the common pattern and the textbook
pattern with a similar difference that exists between the
pictures in textbooks and the child's view of the real world.
Educators have noted recently that many children cannot
identify with the well-scrubbed boys and girls who people
the textbooks and whose fathers and mothers are always
home, helpful, and harmonious. It seems equally certain
that they cannot readily identify either with the artificial
language of the readers.

---

[3] Since the language of elementary textbooks differs so much from
the language of the "prestige dialect," children from culturally deprived
backgrounds have an even more serious problem; that is, in addition to
learning the artificial dialect of the textbook and schoolroom they must
also, if they are to overcome their deprivation, learn the "prestige dialect"
of the community.

The following sentences, taken from a third-grade reader, show that the situation does not improve very much as the child moves on to higher grades:

Sentence 8.10   Through the back yard and up to his room he ran and hopped into bed.

Sentence 8.11   On the ground were the tracks of a chipmunk, but nothing else was stirring.

Sentence 8.12   After the valentine box the children played games.

Structurally, these sentences are very poor examples of literate or oral English. Sentence 8.10 contains two adverbs of motion in the initial position; such adverbs are not usually moved from their normal position following the verb. In Sentence 8.11, there is the strong implication that the tracks of the chipmunk were somehow *stirring*; this is a ludicrous case of artificially flowery writing. Sentence 8.12 also contradicts the linguistic experience of children. Commonly, the preposition *after* introduces an adverbial phrase of time; the sentence, in fact, is not perfectly well formed. Yet these examples are typical, not exceptional. An investigation of almost any third-grade reader will reveal dozens of similar examples. That so many occur is further evidence of the fact that the sentence patterns as well as the vocabulary of readers need to be carefully controlled.

The situation in the high schools is different only in degree rather than kind. Fortunately, some of the literature that high school students read was written by competent authors.[4] Hawthorne, Hemingway, and Mark Twain rarely —if ever—wrote sentences as artificial as those we have just examined. And the students who read the works of these and similar authors can profitably spend time analyzing the structures of their sentences. But the textbooks used to teach grammar are full of artificial patterns and sentences. The following sentences, for example, are all

---

[4] Unfortunately, however, much of the literature in high school textbooks is simplified and bowdlerized. See James J. Lynch and Bertrand Evans, *High School English Textbooks: A Critical Examination* (Boston, Atlantic-Little, Brown, 1963).

taken from a widely used school grammar:

Sentence 8.13 Through his efforts the new building site for the school was purchased.

Sentence 8.14 The dog *lies* on the mat. He *will have lain* there too long by nightfall.

Sentence 8.15 If the newspapers report the matter accurately, we will soon be alarmed because problems are arising among nations.

Like the similar sentences in the elementary textbooks, these sentences do not exist outside the artificial atmosphere of a class in English grammar. No speaker would ever say them. Yet somehow we expect students to become so engrossed by sentences such as these that they develop a fondness for language that is akin to our own.

Or take diagraming. Although some authors admit that diagraming has shortcomings, they nevertheless conclude that diagraming is an aid to understanding sentence structure. But as we have already noted, diagraming reveals only the surface structure of a sentence. Surface structure can frequently be misleading, and may in fact seem entirely arbitrary unless we know the derivational history of the sentence. Consider the example given in Footnote 6 of Chapter 2: *We asked for whoever might be there.* The following diagrams of this sentence are all based on reputable—and current—school grammars:

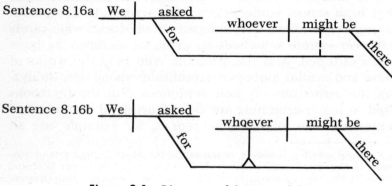

Figure 8.1   Diagrams of Sentence 8.16

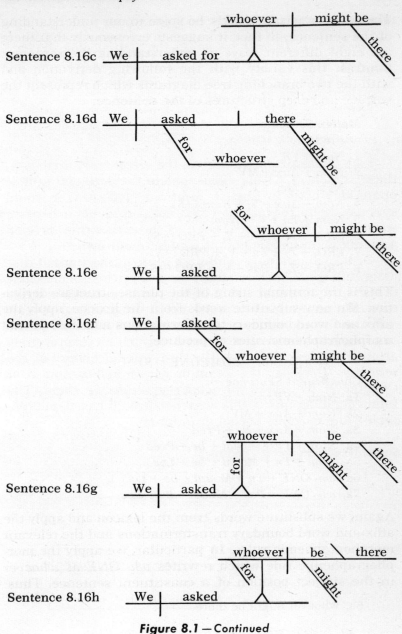

Figure 8.1 — Continued

This variety certainly adds no spice to our understanding of the sentence; in fact, it suggests erroneously that there are eight different ways of understanding the sentence. Contrast this variety with the following derivation and with the two branching tree diagrams which represent the surface and deep structures of the sentence:

Matrix Sentence
    #S#
1. *Nom + VP*
2. *Nom + Aux + MV*
3. *Nom + Aux + V*
4. *Nom + Aux + V_t + Nom (+S)*
5. *Nom + Tn + V_t + Nom (+S)*
6. *PRO_1 + $N^{\underline{o}}$ + Tn + V_t + PRO (+S)*
7. *PRO_1 + Z_2 + Tn + V_t + PRO (+S)*
8. *PRO_1 + Z_2 + Pas + V_t + PRO (+S)*

This is the terminal string of the phrase-structure derivation. We now substitute words from the lexicon, apply the affix and word boundary transformations and the relevant morphographemic rules to produce:

9. *we + asked for + SOMEONE (+S)*

Constituent Sentence
1a. *Nom + VP*
2a. *Nom + Aux + MV*
3a. *Nom + Aux + be + Pred*
4a. *Nom + Tn + Modal + be + Pred*
5a. *Nom + Tn + Modal + be + Loc*
6a. *wh- ONE + Tn + Modal + be + Loc*
7a. *wh- ONE + Pas + Modal + be + Loc*

Again, we substitute words from the lexicon and apply the affix and word boundary transformations and the relevant morphographemic rules. In particular, we apply the morphographemic rule which rewrites *wh- ONE* as *whoever* in the subject position of a constituent sentence. Thus:

8a. whoever might be there.

(This is a **subordinate variant** of the sentence *Someone might be there.*) Then we embed the constituent into the matrix:

10. *we + asked for + SOMEONE (+ whoever + might + be + there).*

The final transformation deletes the PRO form and removes the plus signs and parentheses to give:

11. We asked for whoever might be there.

The branching trees are equally straightforward:

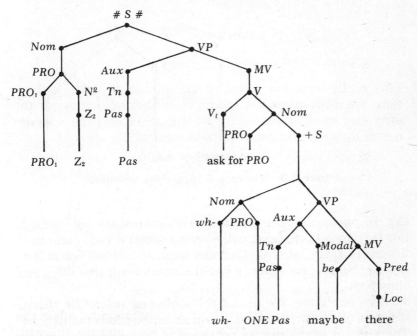

Figure 8.2 Sentence 8.16, deep structure.

Admittedly, even the branching tree diagram of the surface structure is more complex than any of the traditional sentence diagrams. It is also nonarbitrary and more reveal-

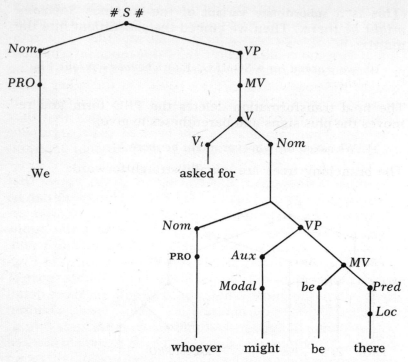

Figure 8.3   Sentence 8.16, surface structure.

ing. In particular, the traditional diagrams are not labeled, nor is there – mathematically – any known way to construct a nonarbitrary labeled diagram similar to traditional diagrams. Notice, however, what the branching tree diagram shows us.

The sentence, *We asked for whoever might be there*, consists of a matrix sentence and an embedded constituent. The subject of the matrix sentence is a pronoun (identified in the deep structure as first-person plural). The verb of the matrix consists of a verb plus a preposition: *ask for*. The verb is in the simple past tense and has, for its direct object, a constituent sentence which has been nominalized. The subject of the constituent sentence is also a pronoun.

The main verb of the constituent is *to be*. There is one auxiliary verb, a modal, which is in the past tense. The predicate of the verb *to be* is a locative adverb: *there*. No traditional diagram could possibly show this much information.

Undoubtedly, only the most advanced students can be taught to construct branching trees. On the other hand, branching trees can be used with great effectiveness by teachers and writers of textbooks. And the fact that they are "right, but complex" cannot be used as an argument that we should retain the methods of traditional diagraming which are, after all, simple but wrong.

Implicit throughout this text has been the notion that the teaching of language and the facts of language can be arranged in a meaningful sequence. The particular sequence would depend, in part, upon whether the pupils are native or nonnative speakers of English. Adult nonnative speakers would probably best begin with the English sentence patterns that most closely resemble those of their native language. They would go into far more detail in some areas (e.g., determiners) than young children whose native language is English. In other areas, (e.g., adjectival modification) they might even be able to proceed more rapidly than young children. These are all promising areas of investigation for linguists, particularly for those who are bilingual.

But much more can be said about a sequence for teaching the facts of language to a native speaker of English. Obviously, we want all pupils to master the basic sentence patterns first. We can reinforce these patterns by using them as the basis for carefully written textbooks. We can conduct more exhaustive analyses of the speech of children at various ages to determine what kinds of variety are introduced into their speech patterns at different times. On the basis of this information, we can construct steps for taking the student from one level of linguistic sophistication to a higher and more effective level. If it proves true— as it almost certainly will—that a pupil acquiring a new derived pattern makes a few stumbling grammatical errors because he has not yet mastered the pattern, we can construct exercises that will help him overcome these errors in the shortest possible time. And perhaps most important, we can encourage the pupil to write naturally. We can compare a pupil's written work with his speech and show him that some differences are merely stylistic, others are the result of stilted and bookish language, and still others are due to the fact that we have time to ponder a written sentence while a spoken sentence — once said — is gone forever. We can, in short, appraise the advantages and disadvantages of both writing and speech for the communication of ideas, emotions, and desires. We can, above all, give the pupil confidence in his ability to speak and write. Once the pupil has this confidence, we can open new and rewarding doors for him.

8.2 GRAMMAR AND LITERATURE

All of these admonitions relate to the first aim of the teacher: explaining the nature of language. The second aim, instilling an awareness of the humanistic values that inhere in the study of English, also relates to grammar.

The notion of linguistic criticism is new and undeveloped. So, too, is the notion of linguistic explication and analysis. Yet both of these areas hold great promise for the student and teacher of English.

Consider a few examples, chosen at random. We have already seen that every imperative sentence in modern English is derived from a kernel with *you* as the subject; in traditional terms, there is a *you* understood, and in transformational terms, there is a *you* in the deep structure. An author can use this understood *you* to establish an immediate and friendly relation with the reader. Melville does just that when he begins *Moby Dick* by writing: "Call me Ishmael." We can even say that literally before the book begins, Melville draws his reader into the story in a manner that is both effective and subtle. The understood *you* also establishes a tone of intimacy which is an important part of the structure of the novel.

We have also noted that the normal place for an adverb
of time is the fourth position, following the verb. Consequently, when such an adverb is moved to the front of a
sentence, it increases our curiosity about what will follow.
And when several adverbs of time are placed in parallel in
front of a sentence, the expectancy increases even more.
Moving adverbs in such a fashion was a favorite device of
Shakespeare in his sonnets:

> When forty winters shall beseige thy brow . . .
>
> *(Sonnet II)*

> When I do count the clock that tells the time,
> And see the brave day sunk in hideous night:
> When I behold the violet past prime,
> And sable curls, all silver'd o'er with white;
> When lofty trees I see barren of leaves,
> Which erst from heat did canopy the herd . . .
>
> *(Sonnet XII)*

> When in disgrace with fortune and men's eyes . . .
>
> *(Sonnet XXIX)*

> When to the sessions of sweet silent thought . . .
>
> *(Sonnet XXX)*

> When I have seen by Time's fell hand defac'd
> The rich-proud cost of outworn buried age;
> When sometime lofty towers I see down-raz'd,
> And brass eternal slave to mortal rage;
> When I have seen the hungry ocean gain
> Advantage on the kingdom of the shore . . .
>
> *(Sonnet LXIV)*

There are many similar constructions, which serve a similar purpose, in Shakespeare's plays.

We can conclude this brief look at the application of
grammatical studies to literature by examining one of the
most effective works in the western world: the opening
chapter of *Genesis* in the King James version of the Bible.

The chapter begins with an adverbial of time: "In the beginning." This is followed by a simple matrix sentence: "God created the heaven." A second direct object is embedded in this matrix. The constituent sentence has the form: "God created the earth." In its final form, then, the first verse consists of an adverbial of time, followed by a sentence containing two direct objects in parallel:

> In the beginning, God created the heaven and the earth.

The subject and verb of the constituent and matrix sentences are identical: "God created . . ." Consequently, they reinforce each other in the final derived sentence; that is, the first verse of *Genesis* doubly emphasizes both God and the act of creation. This is surely an effective use of deep structure.

The remainder of the first chapter of *Genesis* is equally effective. With one exception, each of the following thirty verses is coordinate to the first verse and is introduced with the conjunction *and*. The one exception is verse 27, which is an appositive that reinforces the fact that man is created in God's image:

> So God created man in his *own* image, in the image of God created he him; male and female created he them.

Every other verse, then, except the special one on the creation of man as God's noblest work, is appended in parallel form to the original simple matrix sentence. Structurally—and, as a consequence, also semantically—each additional verse reinforces the power and simplicity of the first verse.

The sentences that relate the story of each day's creation build upon each other in a structural crescendo that reaches its climax with the final verse of the chapter:

> And God saw everything he had made, and behold it was very good. And the evening and the morning were the sixth day.

The first half of this final verse echoes the first verse:

> God created the heaven and the earth. (v. 1)
> God saw everything that he had made. (v. 31)

The subordinate clause, "that he had made," is a nominalization of "God had made everything," which in turn is a restatement of the first verse.

Thus the thirty-one verses of the chapter constitute a kind of circle that ends, structurally, exactly where it began. As T. S. Eliot was later to say in one of his greatest religious poems: "In my beginning is my end." But the latter half of the thirty-first verse changes the basic structure:

> God saw everything that he had made, and behold, it was very good. And the evening and the morning were the sixth day.

This quote includes the first use of the imperative: "behold." As we have seen with Melville, such an imperative draws a reader into the narrative. It also breaks the pattern of development, at the point where it has been rounded out, and adds a quiet coda: "it was very good." The last coordinate sentence reopens the circle and, metaphorically speaking, points the entire progression of matrix and constituent sentences toward infinity. Structurally, therefore, the single long sentence that constitutes the chapter gives the impression of widening out in circles of ever-increasing radius from a center that is the "beginning"; at the same time, the circles seem to turn back upon themselves to reinforce each other. We should notice also how the chapter begins with an adverbial of time and ends with the last of six references to the "day." Thus there is the notion of the circle of time as well as the circle of creation.

In the opinion of the author, it is no hyperbole to say that the first chapter of *Genesis* is a beautiful and dazzling edifice, more elaborate and yet more simple than any building ever constructed, a magnificent linguistic creation that symbolizes in terms of man's greatest invention—language—the creation of the universe itself.

More could obviously be said and much more remains to be done. We have been concerned with a new way of looking at language, and it should come as no surprise that, at the end, we have almost arrived at a new way of looking at the universe. We need not envy the scientists who, perhaps, are ready to open the door to life. Rather, with the tool of language, every teacher of English can open the door to that which is the highest culmination of life: the mind of man.

Discussion

1. What additional reasons can you give in support of teaching language? How do these reasons relate to transformational grammar? Are these reasons implicit in textbooks currently being used to teach language? What tentative answers can you give to the questions raised on p. 208? What kinds of research will be necessary to provide more complete answers?

2. Discuss the relevance of the axiom on p. 209 and its corrolaries to the teaching of English in the elementary and secondary schools and in the colleges and universities.

3. Investigate several textbooks used to teach reading in the elementary and intermediate grades and see what kinds of artificial constructions you are able to find. Compare the sentences in these textbooks with those actually spoken by children, on the basis of **transformational density** (i.e., the number of optional transformations, such as *Q, Emph, Adj,* that occur in a stretch of twenty words).

4. Diagraming is certainly not entirely wrong. For example, a diagram of a simple kernel sentence might be quite revealing. But diagraming is frequently very misleading when the sentences are complicated. Discuss the faults of diagraming, particularly those that might give students erroneous ideas about the structure of sentences.

5. What are some additional ways in which a knowledge of the structure of language can instill an awareness of the humanistic values that inhere in the study of English? How, for example, can a knowledge of structure aid the

teacher in his discussion of such lines as the following:

1. The Grass so little has to do
   I wish I were a Hay—   *(Emily Dickinson)*

2. he sang his didn't he danced his did *(E. E. Cummings)*

3. Some let me tell you of the raven's sins.

(Dylan Thomas)

6. Discuss some of the ways that a knowledge of the structure of language provides a bridge from the academic discipline of English to such other disciplines as anthropology, history, and psychology.

Bibliography

Although an exhaustive bibliography of articles and books in linguistics would fill several volumes, there are only a few items that the teacher of English, in his personal search for a greater understanding of the syntax of his language and of the relationship between syntax and semantics, would find to be immediately useful without a detailed study of linguistic principles. The following highly selective bibliography includes only those items which, in the opinion of the author, the reader of this text could profitably turn to without considerable further study. Some, such as Whorf's book, would present no problems at all. Others, such as Chomsky's articles, are highly technical, but the reader of this book should be able to understand the basic principles being discussed. The technical articles will also give the reader a clearer notion of the kinds of investigations which linguists are making.

ALLEN, HAROLD B., ed., *Readings in Applied English Linguistics*, 2d ed. New York, Appleton-Century-Crofts, 1964. A collection of many important articles, representing the major linguistic "schools," and all concerned—at least indirectly—with the problems of teaching English. The introductions, though brief, are excellent.

BACH, EMMON, *An Introduction to Transformational Grammars*. New York, Holt, Rinehart and Winston, Inc., 1964. A textbook designed to be used in departments of linguistics by students who have completed introductory courses in phonology and morphology. The untrained reader will find many parts of this book difficult, but there are also some relatively simple sections that provide an excellent introduction to the mathematical and logical aspects of transformational theory.

BAUGH, ALBERT C., *A History of the English Language*, 2d ed. New York, Appleton-Century-Crofts, 1957. The standard, one-volume history of the language.

BLOOMFIELD, LEONARD, *Language*. New York, Holt, Rinehart and Winston, Inc., 1933. The major work of the man generally acknowledged to be the founder of modern linguistics in the

United States. Some of Bloomfield's notions are now out of date, but the book still provides an excellent introduction to the study of linguistics.

BLOOMFIELD, MORTON, and Leonard Newmark, *A Linguistic Introduction to the History of English.* New York, Alfred A. Knopf, 1963. A generally successful attempt to combine a history of the language with an introduction to the most basic concepts of linguistics. The authors are particularly successful in defining and illustrating the major "schools" of linguistics.

CHOMSKY, NOAM, "Current Issues in Linguistic Theory" in Fodor, Jerry A., and Jerrold J. Katz, *The Structure of Language.* An extremely difficult, but also extremely important discussion of the theoretical issues with which transformational linguists are concerned. The article is more than a survey, since Chomsky also suggests some answers.

——, "Some Methodological Remarks on Generative Grammar," *Word,* Vol. 17 (August 1961), pp. 219-239. (Also in Allen, Harold B., *Readings in Applied English Linguistics.*) A rebuttal of some criticisms levied against transformational grammar, which concludes with some suggestions for further research. The discussion is technical in some places, but most of this article is not too difficult for teachers of English.

——, *Syntactic Structures.* 's-Gravenhage, The Hague, Mouton & Cie, 1957. The first major publication of the theory of transformational grammar. The theory has since been revised, but this small book will still amply repay the reader's time. As with most of Chomsky's published work, parts of the book are difficult for readers not trained in logic or mathematics, but other parts should present no difficulty.

——, "A Transformational Approach to Syntax," in A. A. Hill, ed., *Proceedings of the Third Texas Conference on Problems of Linguistic Analysis in English, 1958.* Austin, Texas, The University of Texas, 1962. Chomsky's first major paper after the publication of *Syntactic Structures.* He repeats some of the material from his book, but he also adds significant new material, particularly in the form of new phrase-structure and transformational rules. This is one of the least difficult of Chomsky's publications.

FODOR, JERRY A., and Jerrold J. Katz, eds., *The Structure of Language*. Englewood Cliffs, N.J., Prentice-Hall, Inc., 1964. A collection of papers by Chomsky and other leading transformationalists. The papers, most of them written for philosophers and logicians, cover such topics as linguistic theory, grammar, semantics, and the implications for psychologists of the recent advances in linguistic theory.

FRIES, CHARLES CARPENTER, *The Structure of English*. New York, Harcourt, Brace & World, 1952. The major work of a leading structuralist. The transformationalists disagree with the theories that Fries advances, but a knowledge of this book aids in understanding many of the theoretical arguments of the transformationalists. Though difficult in a few places, this book is not beyond the reach of most teachers of English.

JESPERSEN, JENS OTTO, *Essentials of English Grammar*. New York, Holt, Rinehart and Winston, Inc., 1933. One of the major historical grammars of the language. Jespersen's insights and his vast array of examples are still useful.

——, *Language: Its Nature, Development, and Origin*. London, Allen and Unwin, 1922. A classic of historical and comparative scholarship that should be required reading for every linguist and for every teacher connected in any way with the teaching of language.

KATZ, JERROLD J., and Paul M. Postal, *An Integrated Theory of Linguistic Descriptions*. Cambridge, Mass., The M.I.T. Press, 1964. The first significant attempt to combine syntax and semantics in a transformational grammar. Katz and Postal assume a basic knowledge of transformational theory. For most teachers of English, their study will be difficult—though rewarding—reading.

LEES, ROBERT B., *The Grammar of English Nominalizations*. Bloomington, Ind., Research Center in Anthropology, Folklore, and Linguistics, 1960. As indicated throughout this text (particularly in Chapter 4), this study is a detailed analysis of the ways by which speakers of English create new nominals. Though in need of revision, this is still one of the most important—and generally readable—publications by a transformationalist.

———, "Grammatical Analysis of the English Comparative Construction," *Word*, Vol. 17, No. 2 (1961), pp. 171–185. The first detailed transformational analysis of the English comparative construction.

———, "The Grammatical Basis of Some Semantic Notions," in the *Report of the Eleventh Annual Round Table Meeting on Linguistics and Language Studies.* Washington, D.C., Georgetown University Press, 1962. A defense of transformational grammar and a discussion of the notion of modification. Although this study needs to be revised and extended, it is still worthwhile and relatively easy reading.

———, "Some Neglected Aspects of Parsing," *Language Learning*, Vol. 11 (1960), pp. 171–181. (Also in Allen, Harold B., *Readings in Applied English Linguistics.*) A rapid survey of some of the essential features of transformational grammar.

LEHMANN, WINFRED P., *Historical Linguistics: An Introduction.* New York, Holt, Rinehart and Winston, Inc., 1962. A literate and modern survey of a field which is still of great importance in linguistic studies.

MELLON, JOHN C., *A Grammar of English Sentences* (Book One, "The Basic-Sentence Types and their Simple Transformation"; Book Two, "Complex and Conjunctive Transformations"). Culver, Ind., Culver Military Academy, 1964. A textbook intended to be used in the eighth and ninth grades. Mellon is generally quite successful in this attempt to explain to students how the English language operates.

POSTAL, PAUL, *Constituent Structure: A Study of Contemporary Models of Syntactic Description.* Bloomington, Ind., Research Center in Anthropology, Folklore, and Linguistics, 1964. A survey of the techniques and assumptions of the major linguistic "schools." Postal, after a highly technical analysis, concludes that only transformational–generative grammar can adequately describe English.

SAPIR, EDWARD, *Language.* New York, Harcourt, Brace & World, 1921. Like Bloomfield's *Language*, this is the major work of an early and brilliant structuralist. Many linguists feel that Sapir is more relevant to contemporary linguistics than Bloomfield.

SLEDD, JAMES, *A Short Introduction to English Grammar*. Chicago, Scott, Foresman and Company, 1959. An extremely readable "structural grammar," intended for students in the latter years of high school or the early years of college, written by one of the most literate of modern linguists who has since become a leading transformationalist.

———, "Syntactic Strictures," *The English Leaflet*, Vol. 54 (Midwinter, 1961), pp. 14–23. An incisive and witty review of one of the early popularizations of transformational grammar. This is an excellent examination of the problems of introducing transformational grammar into the schools.

SMITH, CARLOTA S., "Determiners and Relative Clauses in a Generative Grammar of English," *Language*, Vol. 40, No. 1 (1964), pp. 37–52. An important, although technical, discussion, with a long "note" on the determiner *the*.

STOCKWELL, ROBERT P., "The Place of Intonation in a Transformational Grammar of English," *Language*, Vol. 36, No. 3 (1960), pp. 360–367. (Also in Allen, Harold B., *Readings in Applied English Linguistics*.) The first attempt to incorporate rules of intonation (i.e., "pitch") into a transformational grammar.

WHORF, BENJAMIN LEE, *Language, Thought, and Reality*. Cambridge, Mass., Technology Press, 1956. A selection of essays from the writings of an early and thought-provoking American linguist. Whorf gives the reader a broad view of the field of linguistics and suggests many ways in which the field interacts with other fields of human inquiry.

Index